Happy Birthday
to Scott.

"There is nothing like a good book". I hope

Love Aunt Heather ×

1987

THE MOUNTIES

THE MOUNTIES

THE HISTORY OF THE ROYAL CANADIAN MOUNTED POLICE

Jim Lotz

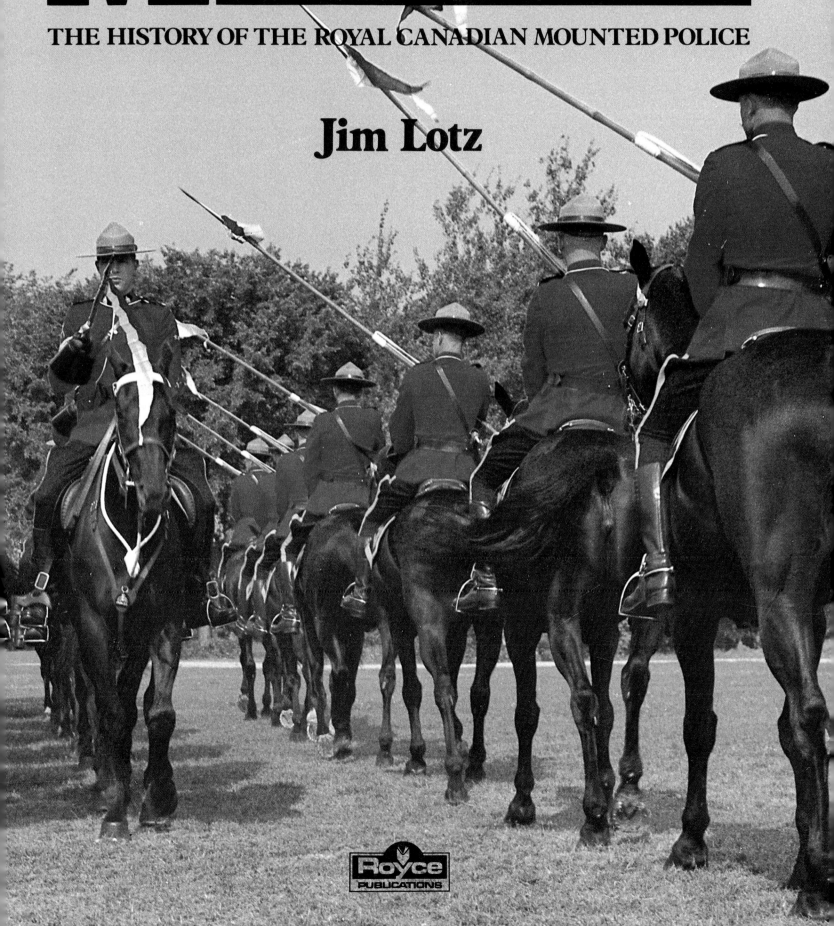

Royce
PUBLICATIONS

DEDICATION

This book is deciated to the memories of Henry Asbjorn Larsen and Robert William Asbil, two members of the Force whose lives touched mine – and enriched it.

First Published in 1984 by Bison Books Corp.
17 Sherwood Place
Greenwich, CT 06830

Copyright © 1984 Bison Books Corp.

ISBN 0 86124 178 9

Printed in Hong Kong

CONTENTS

Chapter 1

THE MOUNTIES – HOLLYWOOD IMAGE AND CANADIAN REALITY

When comedian Dave Broadfoot created Renfrew of the Mounted, the most famous modern member of the RCMP, he made him a corporal. Broadfoot's creation, he admits, is not 'the most qualified or brilliant police officer. He relies for his intellectual guidance on his dog Cuddles . . .,' the sort of companion who would 'run into a burning building and emerge two minutes later with the fire insurance policy wrapped in a wet towel.' Renfrew operates from his office – 'a lonely log cabin on the fourteenth floor of Mountie headquarters' – going to incredible lengths to get his man during episodes of *The Royal Canadian Air Farce*, the radio programme featuring his adventures.

Broadfoot once did his act in RCMP headquarters in Ottawa. In the middle of it Commissioner Simmonds took over the mike, and said: 'Men, we don't have to take this crap from a corporal. From now on it's *Sergeant* Renfrew.' Then he put three stripes on Broadfoot's arm – to wild applause from the assembled Mounties.

Over the past decade, the image of the Royal Canadian Mounted Police has suffered considerably, mainly because of the activities of its Security Service. At Broadfoot's performance, the officer in charge of the evening put the problems of the Force, as its members call it, into perspective: 'You know, gentlemen, looking at the scandals the force has been involved with, looking at our recent past, I'd like to use the words of Pogo – "We have met the enemy and they is us."'

Opposite: The interior of the Royal Canadian Mounted Police chapel at 'Depot' Division in Regina, Saskatchewan.
Above: A guideon – a flag used to show the line of formation of a company – showing the Royal Canadian Mounted Police regimental colours. Also there are patches showing where the RCMP has fought: Northwest Canada 1885: South Africa 1900-2; France & Flanders 1918; Siberia 1918-19; Europe 1939-45.

7

The NWMP's artillery detachment with its two nine-pounder guns was part of the force that established Fort Macleod in 1874.

A New York illustrator visited the Yukon several years ago to gather material to resurrect the Sergeant Preston cartoon strip. The original Mountie had been featured in a radio broadcast from Detroit in 1947, which opened with the sound of ricocheting bullets, the bark of his dog, Yukon King, and the sound of blowing winds. The modern building and operating style of the Force in the Yukon surprised the cartoonist. He 'figured there would be a Mountie in a scarlet uniform with a dog curled up against his legs in front of a fire, smoking a pipe.'

The RCMP became a legend in its own time – a distinct liability in a sceptical age where any form of authority is disliked and distrusted. The last verse of 'The Riders of the Plains,' written in Coburg, Ontario, in July 1878 explains the reasons for founding the Force:

> **Our mission is to plant the right**
> **Of British freedom here –**
> **Restrain the lawless savages,**
> **And protect the pioneer.**
> **And 'tis a proud and daring trust**
> **To hold these vast domains**
> **With but three hundred mounted men –**
> **The Riders of the Plains.**

From its beginnings, the Force favoured the British tradition of understatement. An order posted at Fort Macleod in 1875 set the tone of its public information efforts: 'Nothing concerning the Force or the business of the Force to be in any way discussed with outsiders.' In part this policy was aimed at ensuring that no-one tampered with the administration. But it also earned the RCMP the name 'The Silent Force.' Until fairly recently, the Mounties have made little real effort to tell their story.

And so the myths and legends have grown, untainted by reality. Writing of the Force's activities in the Arctic, Harwood Steele, son of the famous Mountie Sam Steele, noted that the 'heroics of the two-gun, get your man variety,' although well-meant, 'often tended to make the Force ridiculous.' He added: 'Lurid heroics are best avoided, first, because they do not ring true; second, because the men concerned would hate it.'

The image of the Mountie as a kind of solitary knight riding out against evil obviously fills some deep-felt need in all men and women. The members of the Force have always operated at the cutting edge of Canada. Many of the early officers were sons of clergymen who found great satisfaction in bringing law and order to empty lands. But they constantly faced the problems of dealing with the old Adam in human beings – including themselves. In the American West, the 'peacemaker' was a gun, to be used as the first resort. In the Canadian West, the peacemaker was the red-coated Mountie, who used his gun at the last resort.

Hollywood created myths about the Mounties, as did the books, stories and cartoon strips that appeared during the 1920s and 1930s. In 1919, Lasky Studios in Hollywood made a film called *Tyrant Fear*. It showed a Mountie drinking in a brothel, not an unusual occurrence, to judge from the details of diseases in the Force's early annual reports. Protests from Canada forced the studio to withdraw the film, and it was censored in Britain.

The Force's reports are factual, precise and unemotional, reflecting the organization's style. The introduction to a history of the RCMP that appeared in 1954, however, hinted at the ambiguity that marks all police work.

The Mounted Police differ very little in essence from the athletes in armour who rode out from King Arthur's Court bent on redressing human wrongs. Although if you told a harassed constable who was writing a report of some violation of the Meat and Canned Foods Act that he was today's Sir Lancelot, he might snort.

The RCMP celebrated its centennial in 1973, just as the first revelations of the wrongdoings of its Security Service emerged. One book celebrating the event mentions a young constable who died in a vicious winter storm in the Arctic in 1903. In a pocket of his scarlet tunic was found a note: 'Lost, horse dead. Am trying to push ahead. Have done my best.' This last message, the author states, 'seems to typify the spirit of the whole force.' The Force's Roll of Honour makes no mention of a death in the Arctic in 1903. And even Sergeant Renfrew would think twice about travelling on horseback in the Arctic in winter. Like many other similar stories, this one is apocryphal.

Over the past few years, a number of books have tried to puncture the Mountie myths. Their titles convey their biases – *The RCMP vs The People, Nobody Said No, The Crimes of the Secret Police (Les Crimes de la Police Montée)*. One book by two sociology professors ascribes the misdeeds of the Mounties to 'official deviance,' 'role strain,' and 'status anguish.' The authors ask the readers to report any wrongdoing by the RCMP or any other Canadian police force to them: 'Confidentiality of sources will be completely respected.'

A left-wing writer describes the RCMP as 'a paramilitary cavalry force mobilized over 100 years ago to end communal ownership of the prairie lands, to crush Indian-Métis resistance to the encroachments of the railway interests, to open up the West to white settlement . . .'

The Force's officers are 'thorough-going and vicious reactionaries . . . blatantly anti-labor and pro-capitalist . . .' On the other hand, a TV comedy writer who put together a comedy about the Mounties, when asked what he found funny about the RCMP replied, 'That red uniform, the baggy pants, the Smokey the Bear hat and the proud image.'

The role of the RCMP cannot be seen outside the stream of Canadian history and present-day society. The Force, a social invention of the central government, brought order out of frontier chaos. It did this in a number of ways, although until recently its members were underpaid, overworked, badly housed and subject to the whims of politicians who almost abolished the Force on several occasions. Only 35,000 men wore the scarlet and the gold during the first century – about twice the number of the present establishment of the Force. Among this number were heroes and cowards, honest men and villains. But the vast majority were ordinary men who learned how to combine initiative with a strong sense of discipline. On Canada's frontier the Mounties anticipated problems, and took effective steps to prevent them from becoming crises. In doing so they developed an *esprit de corps*, and became an élite body. In 1949, 6000 men applied to join the Force – and only 600 were accepted.

As the RCMP became older and larger, it lost the flexibility that marked its early style and became more rigid and bureaucratized. By the early 1970s, it had 4500 regulations. When a Cape Bretoner joined the Force in 1964, the recruiting officer told his mother, 'We take a boy and give you back a man.' This recruit's uncle had been a Mountie, and had enthralled his nephew with the effect the uniform had on women – 'He called it scarlet fever.'

Special constables of Indian descent are trained at the Royal Canadian Mounted Police Academy – 'Depot' Division, Regina, Saskatchewan. The new RCMP has both men and women special constables.

Left: The dress uniform of a North West Mounted Police constable in the year 1877.

Right: A constable in his uniform with pith helmet – The NWMP dress uniform of about 1877.

Left: A NWMP constable's dress uniform – 1901
Right: A constable in RNWMP dress uniform – 1905

Above: A sergeant of the Royal Canadian Mounted Police in Review Order of Dress (1973) in front of the Maple Leaf.

This particular individual found the training and the socialization process through which recruits are put in Regina too much for him, and left the Force to become a hairdresser. The aim of the training of any elité group is to impress on those who join it that the organization is more important than the individuals who comprise it. In 1976, the Marin Royal Commission on 'Public Complaints, Internal Discipline and Grievance Procedure Within the Royal Canadian Mounted Police' concluded that the excessively rigid, centralized, and formal disciplinary system of the Force led to 'resentment and bitterness' in the lower ranks. In 1977, the McDonald Royal Commission began its enquiries into the excesses of the RCMP. Over the next four years, at a cost of $15 million, this commission sorted through the allegations against the Force. It concentrated on what the Mounties had done wrong – not on what they had done right. In May 1980 a member of the Force committed suicide after giving testimony.

The McDonald Commission report stated: 'The RCMP through its recruiting, training and management practises, engulfs its members in an ethos akin to that found in a monastery or a religious order.'

The recent attacks on the Force do not appear to have destroyed its credibility, or the public's faith in it. Its 'monastic' style lies at the basis of all police work, and the values that the Force enshrines – discipline, courage, group loyalty and respect for tradition – lie very close to the heart of the Canadian lifestyle.

Generally speaking, Canadians are a law-abiding people.

But the police know that violence lies latent just below the surface of even the mildest individuals. The police have to operate in ambiguous situations when the public want order, but don't like authority. Most people try to have as little to do with the police as possible. But when they need a policeman they want him at once. Society often sanctions the ends of policing, but denies the means. The Chairman of the McDonald Commission, a judge in Alberta, authorized police to bug private premises – but refused to allow them to enter the premises surreptitiously to install the microphones.

Over the past two decades, rapid social change has removed from individuals the ability to control their own destinies. Demands for freedom and liberation have arisen, and there has been an increasing emphasis on human rights rather than on the individual's responsibility to society. The person who breaks the rules, the outlaw, the underdog, the criminal, has received a great deal of public sympathy at the expense of the person who enforces the law. And the victims of crime are often forgotten. In recent years, more attention is being paid to understanding the difficulties of policing society – and the impact of crime upon victims. W S Gilbert captured the essence of police work when he wrote:

**'When constabulary duty's to be done, to be done,
The Policeman's lot is not a happy one.**

Police work is lonely, and usually monotonous. The quiet patrolling is interspersed with bursts of action and moments of sheer terror. The police can rely only on each

Below: **Photographing the results of a test-fired cartridge at the RCMP's Crime Detection Laboratories in Ottawa.**

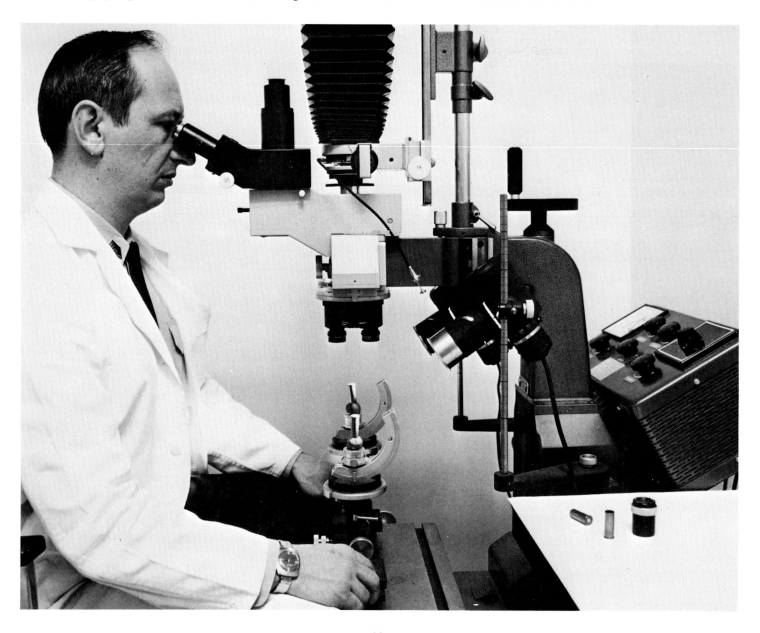

Above: In the enforcement of the 'Small Vessels' Act, Mounties often have to examine the safety equipment of pleasure craft.

Below: One of the most important skills to be developed at the RCMP Academy 'Depot' Division is that of self-defence.

other, and the camaraderie apparent in detachment offices does something to offset the constant feelings of tension and threat. Heavy drinking, divorce and suicide among policemen are part of the price they pay for maintaining law and order.

Like most Canadians I have had little contact with the RCMP. They proved to be excellent informants when I did research in the Yukon and Cape Breton Island. But first hand contact with their work came only a few years ago, when I served on a committee on highway safety. For two evenings I accompanied RCMP officers on highway patrol to see how things looked from the front seat of a police car. From four in the afternoon until midnight, we cruised the highways – and a few of the byways – with the radar scanner flickering. Once in a while, the Mountie would see something, turn the car, and roar off after a traffic offender. Usually they let them off with a warning about some minor infraction of the law. Like the trained professionals they were, the officers had a sixth sense about who was breaking the law. They had stopped offenders before I realized that an offence had taken place. Late at night, on the empty highway, every dark shadow or moving form exuded menace. One evening we lay in wait for speeders to roar down a stretch of highway – and nothing happened.

On another occasion, a routine breathalyzer check suddenly became dangerous. A car slowed as it approached the road block, then suddenly accelerated, almost hitting the officer directing the traffic. He jumped into his car, roared off, and was back with the driver in minutes. He

Far left: A laboratory technician types blood at the RCMP's Crime Laboratory's Serology Section. The information obtained from this system is then used to compare the blood type of a suspect or a victim of crime to blood stains found at the scene of that crime.
Above left: An RCMP Jet Ranger helicopter – 1973.
Center left: An RCMP Motorcycle Highway Patrolman and his son.
Opposite: The badge of the Royal Canadian Mounted Police with the Queen's Crown, showing the motto: 'Mantiens le Droit.'
Below: Checking thumb prints at the RCMP Crime Laboratory in Ottawa.

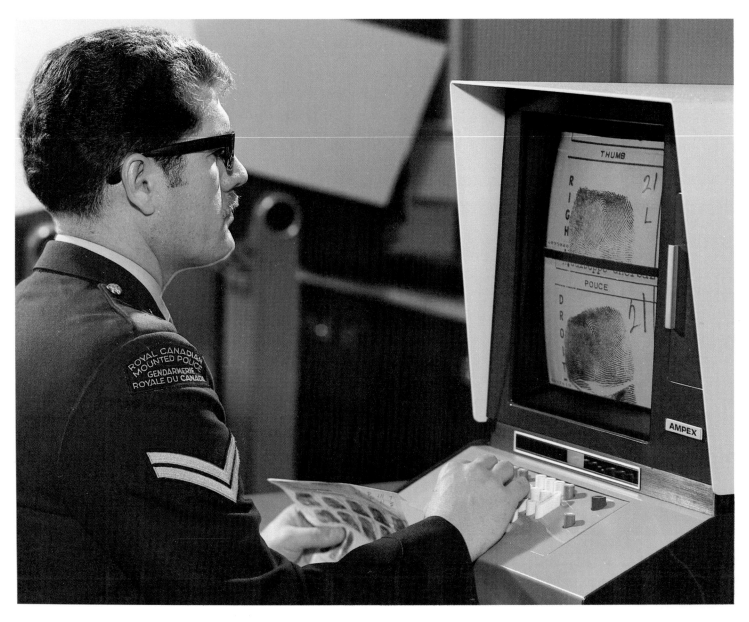

turned out to be a man with his 14 year old son. Drunken drivers come in all shapes and sizes. This one, after a burst of aggression, turned passive and silent. He took the breathalyzer test in the van, but the Mountie found that the machine was not working so we went back to use the equipment at the detachment office. The man failed the test and was charged. Then the Mountie drove him and his son home.

Throughout Canada, the Force carries out a wide range of duties. In 1983, the drug squad in Montreal seized 14 tons of marijuana; in Inverness County, Cape Breton, Mounties investigated the death of a youth thrown to the ground when a load of hay upon which he was sitting shifted; in Ottawa, the Force opened a file on the Animal Liberation Front which was raiding fur stores, meat plants and animal laboratories. A Mountie accompanied Prince Andrew on his canoe trip down the Nahanni River in the Northwest Territories, and in Sault Ste Marie the Force completed a case when a car dealer was fined $2200 for tampering with odometers. When an Air Canada Boeing 767 which ran out of fuel skidded to a halt at Gimli, Manitoba, members of the local detachment were on the spot to help. Other Mounties took photographs of the crowd as Prince Charles opened the new Ottawa police station, removed demonstrators from the Peace Tower, and searched the home of an author who interviewed a former Mountie who passed information to the Russians. In Saskatchewan members of the Force tried to keep order when a rock group failed to appear as scheduled, and in British Columbia they formed a special squad to track down sexual attackers of children and tried to find out why someone had placed a bomb on a plane and killed two men.

The Force also complained that they lacked the resources to tackle the $10 billion drug trade in Canada, an

Above: Mounties need to maintain a friendly working relationship with the public and they also have a function of teaching safety to the young. Here a policewoman stops her patrol car to have a chat with a young girl.
Right: Two members of the RCMP conducting an investigation at the site of a simulated motor vehicle accident.

Above: An aerial view of the Royal Canadian Mounted Police Training Academy at 'Depot' Division, Regina, Saskatchewan, 1976.

'industry' about the same size as General Motors in Canada.

As they went about these tasks, members may have recalled some of the heroic episodes of the Force's 110 year history – James Walsh walking into Sitting Bull's camp, Sam Steele laying down the law during the Klondike Gold Rush, Henry Larsen roaring hymns as the *St Roch* ploughed through Arctic storms. They might also remember Francis Dickens abandoning Fort Pitt, Leif Crozier leading his men into a Métis ambush at Duck Lake, and Frank Fitzgerald and the other three men of the Lost Patrol, struggling to reach Fort McPherson, dying as they went.

Closer to our times, the Force lost Constable Hoey in 1958 – killed while investigating a complaint at Botwood, Newfoundland – and Constable Lepine who died in a car accident near Whalley, British Columbia, in 1962 while on duty.

They would certainly remember an incident in Calgary in 1981. The RCMP, acting on a tip, trailed an escaped murderer as he left a house. As they closed in on the man, city police arrived, and fired 10 to 15 shots – wounding the criminal and RCMP Sergeant Ray Forsythe.

Dave Broadfoot claims that Sergeant Renfrew is popular with Canadians because he 'humanizes the image of the Mountie.' In recent years, the Force has been reaching out towards the Canadian community, seeking to be part of it. It is shedding its air of aloofness and becoming more accessible and approachable to the public. In doing so, it need not fear for its reputation. In many places, and at many times, the history of the Force has been that of Canada.

And both the strengths and the failings of the Royal Canadian Mounted Police offer us a chance to see ourselves and this country more clearly. It's in this spirit that this history has been written.

Chapter 2

THE MAKING OF THE FORCE – THE MARCH WEST, 1874

At 5 pm on 8 July 1874, a two mile long column of the North West Mounted Police left Dufferin on Manitoba's Red River to bring law and order to the Canadian West.

The Mounties were created by Sir John A Macdonald, Canada's first prime minister, as part of his policy of national development. South of the border lawless men moved into the open west after the American Civil War ended in 1865. During the first week of the Sioux War of 1868, 700 whites died and 200 were taken prisoner. Keeping the peace in the west was costing Washington $20 million a year.

Macdonald decided that the law would precede the influx of settlers into the territories that Canada had acquired from the Hudson's Bay Company in 1870. And those who brought law and order to the new Dominion's new lands would be under the control of the central government – not subject to the whims of the local people as they were south of the border.

A federal presence would prevent the annexation of the new territories by the expanding United States. And disturbing reports had reached Ottawa about conditions among the Indians of southern Alberta. Here American whisky traders had built forts, debauching the Indians with 'Whoop-Up bug juice,' named for the strongest post. The traders also sold the Indians modern repeating rifles with which they slaughtered the huge herds of buffalo, the lynchpin of their existence. From the Indians, the traders took buffalo robes, wolf and fox skins – and horses.

Above: A constable of the North West Mounted Police (1866) – a painting by G E McElroy.
Opposite: NWMP members of the Ten Mile Detachment (with their dogs), 1891.

In 1870-71, Lieutenant Butler of the British Army travelled 3000 miles across what he called 'The Great Lone Land,' Canada's Northwest Territories. Here he reported, you could 'wander for five hundred miles in a direct line without seeing a human being' and the 'institutions of Law and Order' were 'wholly unknown.'

In 1870, Manitoba had become a province, and Macdonald recognized that the empty west would attract settlers. But he did not want to upset the Americans by a display of military might. Yet the Indians had to be overawed and kept under control. And they also had to be protected from the exploitation of outsiders.

In 1872, Alexander Morris, lieutenant governor of Manitoba, demanded that Canada 'stable its elephant.' Yet the prime minister dragged his feet until 3 May 1873, when the bill to establish the North West Mounted Police passed through the House of Commons without opposition. Macdonald wanted a force with the authority of the police, backed by the power of the military. He examined the operations of the Royal Irish Constabulary and the Indian Army, and hoped to combine aspects of both. He considered, but discarded, the name 'North West Mounted Rifles.' The Act that created the force summarizes its duties as preserving peace, preventing crime and apprehending criminals. Its members would also act as court orderlies, jailers, customs officers and escorts for prisoners and lunatics. In their oath of office, the Mounted Policemen promised to perform their duties 'without fear, favour or affection of or towards any person or party whatsoever.'

Macdonald pointed out that the members of the new force would act as customs inspectors, and thus contribute to government income. And every officer would be a Justice of the Peace so that summary justice could be dispensed without an elaborate system of courts. On 30 August 1873, Governor General Lord Dufferin signed the Order-in-Council that brought the North West Mounted Police formally and legally into being.

The need for such a force was brought home as details of the Cypress Hills Massacre filtered into Ottawa. In the spring of 1873, Assiniboine Indians camped near Solomon's and Farwell's trading posts, about 100 miles southwest of the site of Swift Current, Saskatchewan. Wolfers returning south to Montana also rested at Farwell's post: Wolfers killed wolves (and the dogs of Indians) with poisoned buffalo meat. Cree Indians had stolen 40 horses belonging to the group who had lost their trail in the Cypress Hills. Their scouts found the Assiniboine camp – but not the horses. On the following day, a man at the trading post, who had retrieved his stolen horse only to find it missing when he woke up, led the Wolfers in a raid on the Indian camp. Shooting broke out, and at least 20 Indians and one white man died. After the killings, the Wolfers destroyed the Indian camp.

To Indians, stealing horses rated as a sport; to whites, it was a hanging matter. South of the border, the battle was hailed as a victory over a dangerous enemy. In Canada it was viewed as a slaughter of innocents. The Mounties later

Original uniforms of the Force – 1874. Seated is Inspector John French. The bearded officer, second from right, is Inspector F J Dickens, son of the novelist Charles Dickens.

Left: Commissioner George Arthur French, 1873-76.
Below: Lt Col W Osborne Smith.

Previous pages: During the March West, the RCMP harvested prairie grass to be used as fodder.

tried to convict the whites involved in the massacre, but all were acquitted because of lack of evidence. The actual massacre site is closed to visitors, but Solomon's and Farwell's posts have been reconstructed to convey the feel of life on the western frontier in the 1870s.

The Cypress Hills Massacre forced Macdonald to act.

Recruiting began for the new police force, and plans were made to send an expedition to stamp out the whisky trade. The members of the NWMP had to be 'of sound constitution, able to ride, active and able bodied, of good character and between the ages of eighteen and forty years.' They had to be able to read and write either French or English. The men signed on for three years, after which time they could obtain a land grant of 160 acres in the Northwest Territories. Most of the officers had had military experience; one had fought with the Papal Zouaves in Italy, and another had served in the Confederate Army. The third son of Charles Dickens, nicknamed 'Chicken-stalker' by his family, received a commission in November 1874.

The first permanent commanding officer or commissioner, Lieutenant-Colonel George Arthur French, a gunner born in Ireland, had been educated at British military establishments before joining the Royal Artillery in 1860. A strict disciplinarian, energetic and able, French also showed great concern for his men.

Pay for constables was $1 a day, 75 cents for subconstables, and the desire for adventure motivated most of those who joined the first contingents. Fred Bagley en-

listed in 1874 at 15, inspired by the books of James Fenimore Cooper. He thought that life in the NWMP would be 'one grand round of riding wild mustangs, chasing whisky traders and horse thieves, potting noble savages, and hobnobbing with haughty Indian Princes and lovely sophisticated Princesses.' A few years in the force, however, he added, 'sufficed to dissipate much of this glamour.'

Of the first 150 recruits, nine were farmers, 46 clerks, 13 police or military, and 43 skilled workers. Thirty-nine were classified as 'miscellaneous or no previous experience.' Politicians submitted lists of job seekers, but the standards of the new organization, the calibre of the officers and the conditions of service soon weeded out the unfit and the unworthy. When Dick Steele fell from his horse, and was knocked out cold, the riding instructor ordered two recruits to 'get that clumsy fellow out of here' and went on with the training. The instructor, Steele's brother Sam, had been the third man into the force when he signed on at Lower Fort Garry on 3 November 1873.

Sir John A Macdonald wanted 'as little gold lace, fuss and feathers' as possible as far as the uniform was concerned. But to impress the Indians, and to show the link with the Imperial Army that had been a power and a presence during the Riel Rebellion of 1870, the Mounties wore scarlet tunics; this also distinguished them from the blue-clad US Cavalry. Full dress uniform included white helmet, white gauntlet gloves and shining black boots into which were tucked steel-grey breeches. Later the helmets were replaced by pillbox hats. This rig proved completely unsuited to conditions out west, and on patrol the Mounties dressed informally. They wore the slouch hat well before the stiff-brimmed Stetson became official issue in 1901.

The men looked magnificent, especially when seated on bay horses. But these animals died in scores on the Great March West that began on 8 July 1874; the recruits would have travelled better on mules or Indian ponies. And their standard rifle, the Snider-Enfield Mark III single shot carbine, was markedly inferior to the repeating rifles used by the Indians. Many of the first batch of revolvers the Mounties received arrived badly damaged.

The column of route that left Dufferin comprised six divisions, mounted on variously coloured horses. Three divisions had been formed at Lower Fort Garry, and they had been joined by three others recruited in eastern Canada. In December 1873, Commissioner French sent out the first Mountie patrol to arrest whisky traders selling their wares to Indians on the west coast of Lake Winnipeg.

The eastern divisions had assembled and trained on the Toronto lakefront, on the site of the present Canadian National Exhibition grounds, in the spring of 1874. They entrained on 6 June for the West, dressed in civilian clothes for the journey through the United States. Some, afraid of being scalped, had shaved their heads and were jeered at as jailbirds. Fred Bagley's mother advised him to say his prayers regularly, and a father told his son that he would rather hear of his death than his dishonour. When the recruits from Toronto reached Dufferin on 19 June, they were greeted by a prairie thunderstorm. Hailstorms flattened their tents. Great sheets of lightning and peals of thunder stampeded the horses, and some reached Grand Forks, North Dakota, 60 miles away, before being recaptured.

For William Parker, son of an English clergyman, who had joined the Force in preference to working on a farm, the departure from Dufferin was far from glamorous. Instead of sitting on a fine bay horse, he had to drive a yoke of oxen pulling an ammunition wagon. Just outside Dufferin, the animals took off at full gallop. Two 'half breeds' stopped them, and took over Parker's task while the Mountie hoofed it back to camp and retrieved his charger.

Parker found the prairie 'enchanting.' But the Force suffered its first casualties when two men, left behind at Dufferin with typhoid and malaria, died. Parker fell ill on the first night, became quite helpless by the time the expedition reached La Roche Percée just beyond the borders of Manitoba, and was sent back to Dufferin with typhoid fever caused by drinking tainted water. At La Roche Percée, one division under Inspector Jarvis headed north on an epic journey to Edmonton.

The rest of the column staggered on.

The impracticality of this mode of travel soon became apparent. In later years when Jarvis regaled the Reverend John McDougall, a Methodist missionary, with a 'very fiery description' of the journey west, the clergyman pointed out that the Métis farmers/traders/hunters did the trip three times each summer – 'with no government behind them.'

American newspapers claimed that the column had been wiped out by Indians, and in eastern Canadian churches prayers were said for its safety. On 10 July, 12 deserters vanished over the border. Riders went ahead searching for sweet grass and clean water, and wagons, cattle and oxen often failed to catch up with the main column in the evening, so the men did without food. Soggy bread and salt bacon, supplemented by flapjacks fried in axle grease, formed the staple of the Mountie's diet; one man sprinkled machine oil on his food to improve the flavour.

At the first church service on the trail, on 27 July, some Mounties suggested the need for prayer 'for there is no other way we will reach our journey's end alive.' Uniforms torn and dusty, ribs sticking out from lack of food, the Mounties became obsessed with the quest for water. Often it was a black liquid that caused dysentery. And when the men found the waterholes, the mosquitoes found them. The horses could not carry their riders, who walked beside them. The Mounties also hauled wagons and guns up hills because the horses and oxen were too weak.

The triumphal march west became a nightmare.

On 12 August the column encountered 30 Sioux – 'a most wretched lot' of 'Sooty Sons of the Plains.' Early in September, the Mounties sampled their first buffalo – old bulls too tough for most of the men to swallow.

Finally, on 9 September, they reached the meeting place of the Bow and Belly Rivers. Here they expected to find Fort Whoop-Up, the centre of the whisky trade they had come to suppress. Instead they could see only three broken-down, roofless huts.

To add to their other problems the Mounties were now lost.

On the following day, the weather turned very cold and wet, and the officers and men gave up their blankets to cover the horses at night. Despite this, a dozen animals died of cold as they struggled toward the Sweetgrass Hills on the American border.

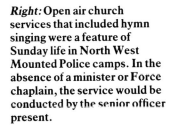

Right: Open air church services that included hymn singing were a feature of Sunday life in North West Mounted Police camps. In the absence of a minister or Force chaplain, the service would be conducted by the senior officer present.

Chapter 3
ENCOUNTER AT FORT WHOOP-UP

While the expedition rested, Commissioner French and Assistant Commissioner Macleod struck off in mid-September for Fort Benton, Montana, the 'Chicago of the Plains,' the regional transportation centre at the head of navigation of the Missouri and home base of the whisky traders. On their return with clothes, supplies, fresh horses and news, the Commissioner split the expedition in two. One group under French returned to Dufferin. The rest, under Macleod, headed for Fort Whoop-Up to confront the whisky traders.

Macleod had recruited a guide in Fort Benton, the first of many Métis and Indians to serve the Force over the years. Jerry Potts, son of a white father and an Indian mother, had grown up half-wild among the Indians of the American West, and killed his first man in a drunken brawl in Montana. His mother had been murdered by a Blood Indian in 1872; Potts tracked the man to Canada and shot him. A small, bow-legged, laconic man, the guide had an uncanny feel for the country, an unfailing sense of direction, and a colossal thirst.

Potts led Macleod and the Mounties over the hills towards Fort Whoop-Up. When asked what was over the next hill, he replied 'Nudder hill.'

Finally, the column crossed the last hill.

From a bluff above the place where the St Mary River met the Oldman in what is now south-western Alberta, the Mounties looked down upon a strongly-built fort and prepared for action.

Above: Guide and interpreter Jeremy Potts was hired by Assistant Commissioner Macleod to lead the NWMP to Fort Whoop-Up, a suspected center of illegal whiskey trading near present-day Lethbridge, Alberta. He served with the Force for many years and was the interpreter at the signing of Treaty Number 7.
Opposite: Fort Whoop-Up.

Jerry Potts, standing at center, was an interpreter and scout for the North West Mounted Police.

Built of massive logs and earth, with two bastions and loopholes in its mud-chinked walls, Fort Whoop-Up flew a flag combining the Stars and Stripes and the insignia of its owners above its sturdy oak gates. To the right of the gate were three small wickets. Through them Indians pushed buffalo skins in exchange for trade goods and 'fire water.' The liquid, made by adding tabasco, vitriol, red pepper, ginger, tobacco juice, molasses and even ink to watered whisky, drove Indians into drunken frenzies.

In the early days of free trading north of the Missouri, Americans simply entered Indian camps to sell their wares. But when the Indians drank, or felt they had been cheated, they took the traders' goods – and often their lives. As American troops stopped the liquor traffic south of the border, the traders moved north into Canada, and built a string of forts including Whoop-Up, Slideout, Robbers' Roost and Whisky Gap. Fort Whoop-Up, built by John Healy and A B Hamilton, had been a collection of shacks connected by a picket fence when first erected in 1869. It had been burned down by drunken Indians almost as soon as it was completed. The fort upon which the Mounties gazed had been completed in 1871, at a cost of $25,000. Healy and Hamilton had netted $50,000 on their first trip into Blackfoot country, and their trading post had the look of permanence.

Staveley Hill, a British financier and Member of Parliament who travelled in the west in the 1880s, lamented: 'Oh, my Hudson's Bay Company! All this might have been yours, if you had not sat by with folded arms and allowed your own legitimate business to have been grabbed by some Montana adventurers.' In Canada, the Indians, valued as partners with the Bay in the fur trade, established long term relationships with the traders. South of the border, Indians occupied land coveted by settlers, and battled newcomers to their territories. The American free traders saw themselves as harbingers of civilization, claiming to be teaching the Indians how to behave, and so making the country safe for travel and settlement.

The 'Buffalo Indians' relied entirely on that huge beast for clothing, food, shelter, equipment and identity. Living in small groups, sharing a deep religious faith that assured them of their place in an orderly cosmos, the members of the Blackfoot Confederacy were passing through a crisis when the Mounties reached the West. In the previous century they had obtained guns from the Cree to the north, and horses from the Shoshone to the south. These acquisitions sealed their doom, for it enabled them to hunt and kill the buffalo much more efficiently. Then, in the middle of the 19th century, came traders to buy the buffalo skins. In exchange they provided repeating rifles and a variety of vile concoctions masquerading as whisky.

The Reverend John McDougall wrote of scores of thousands of buffalo robes and hundreds of thousands of wolf and fox skins and the best horses being taken south to Montana. With their possessions went the pride and dignity of the people. 'Within a few miles of us, that winter of 1873/4, forty-two able-bodied men . . . were slain in drunken rows . . . There was no law but might . . . whole camps went on the spree . . . shooting, stabbing, killing, freezing, dying,' noted McDougall.

As the Mounties made their painful way west in the summer of 1874, Father Scollen, another missionary, reported to Lieutenant-Governor Laird in Winnipeg that he had travelled among the Blackfoot: 'It is painful to me to see the state of poverty to which they have been reduced. Formerly, they had been the most opulent Indians in the country, now they were clothed in rags without horses and without guns.'

As he looked over Fort Whoop-Up, Macleod wondered what to do. He'd been told that the Canadian west swarmed with American desperadoes and drunken Indians. Yet the fort looked strangely silent.

He asked Jerry Potts' advice.

'Just ride in,' suggested the scout. The two men cantered to the massive gates, and Macleod pounded on them. This style of direct action marked the Mounties' approach to many problems in the future.

The gates opened.

But only one man greeted the newcomers – a gaunt, uncouth individual named Dave Akers. The fort was empty, he informed Macleod. But if he cared to bring his men inside, he could offer them a feast of buffalo meat and fresh vegetables from the fort garden. Inside Fort Whoop-Up, the Mounties marvelled at the spacious quarters and comforts of the place. They searched everywhere, but could find no whisky.

The traders had decamped south of the border when they learned of the approach of the Mounties. They were frontier businessmen, intent on quick profits, who knew that their trade was a dying one – literally and metaphorically. Whisky was killing off their customers and guns the buffalo. In his reminiscences of life in the Mounties, Cecil Denny stated that he found the traders 'a very decent lot of men in spite of all we had heard against them.'

A sense of anticlimax pervaded the column as it quit Fort Whoop-Up. Geared for a fight, they had been met by a silent fort in an empty land. Yet the march west had created an *esprit de corps* among the members of the new force. And it had weeded out the weaklings. When recruits complained of saddlesores, they received salt to rub on them to form calluses. 'We became so tough I could sit on a prickly pear,' reported one Mountie.

Jerry Potts led the Mounties to a place on the Oldman River. Here, surrounded by good grass for the horses and trees for building and fuel, they built a fort and named it for Macleod. Shortly afterwards, Macleod received word of whisky traders. A troop of Mounties rode out, raided the camp, confiscated the whisky, arrested the five traders and brought them back to Fort Macleod. Here they were tried, found guilty and heavily fined.

By the end of 1874, the Mounted Police had six posts in the west. About half were stationed in and around Manitoba, at Dufferin, Swan River, Winnipeg and Fort Ellice. Twenty-two guarded the northern plains from Edmonton, and 150 officers and men garrisoned Fort Macleod.

Jerry Potts played a vital role in maintaining good relations with the Indians. He visited the tribes of the Blackfoot Confederacy, explaining to the chiefs that the Mounties had come to protect them. Embittered by encounters with the United States Cavalry, the hated 'Long Knives,' the Indians agreed to remain neutral and to leave the newcomers alone.

But they kept a close eye on them.

Then Jerry Potts brought three chiefs to Fort Macleod to meet the commander. Soon others came to visit. Macleod smoked the peace pipe with them, respected their rituals and their prayers, reassured them about the police's presence in the country and dealt fairly with them. The police had come to teach the Indians the law, Macleod said, and anyone who broke it, white or Indian, would be punished. He became good friends with Crowfoot, chief of the Blackfoot Confederacy, who called him Stamix Otokan (Bull's Head). Thus was laid the basis for mutual trust and respect that marked relationships between Indians and Mounties as they weathered a difficult decade together.

During the first winter, members of the new body patrolled the prairies, seeking out whisky traders, recovering stolen horses and making contact with Indian bands. They froze their faces, lost their way and suffered incredible hardships while living in primitive conditions.

In his diary for February 1875, Sergeant Antrobus wrote about a storm 'such as is seen only on the prairies' arising. The party sought shelter; 'Imagine two or three men lying in the snow behind a bush, shivering like leaves . . .' These men were luckier than Constables Wilson and Baxter, 'two gentlemen from a good family.' They left Fort Macleod on New Year's Eve, 1874, despite suggestions that they overnight there. As the Ottawa *Free Press* put it, 'they thought they were all right and knew the way' to Fort Kipp. A blizzard arose, and on the following afternoon their horses came home – saddled and riderless. Wilson, 'not quite dead,' expired ten minutes after being found, and Baxter, 'lying in a snow heap quite dead,' was found on the next night.

In May 1875, Inspector J M Walsh built the fort named after him in the Cypress Hills. It was 'nicely situated in a valley surrounded by wooded hills,' and soon a small settlement grew up around it, complete with trading stores operated by Fort Benton merchants, a billiard hall, a hotel restaurant and barber shop. It remained the headquarters of the NWMP until the spring of 1883 when Regina took over that function and Fort Walsh was demolished.

Fort Walsh has been reconstructed as a historic site.

About 200 miles to the west lay Fort Macleod, in the shadows of the Rockies. The Mounties formed a thin red line across Blackfoot Country. They could not hope to fight the Indians and win. So their relations with them followed a very different pattern from those south of the border.

North West Mounted Police on parade at Medicine Hat, Alberta, in 1875.

Chapter 4
CONFRONTING SITTING BULL

Between 1875 and 1885 the Mounties served as an instrument of Ottawa's Indian policy. This had three thrusts – signing treaties under which the Indians ceded their lands to the crown, settling the bands on reserves and turning them into self-sufficient farmers.

The Mounties had also to deal with an influx of battle-weary Sioux from the the United States. And rising discontent among the Métis led to the outbreak of the second Riel Rebellion in which a number of Cree joined.

By 1875, the Dominion Government had acquired title to all lands between Manitoba and British Columbia, which had entered Confederation in 1871. Only the lands claimed by the Saskatchewan Indians and the tribes of the Blackfoot Confederacy had not been secured for Canada. A few Indians wandered the boreal forests of the North, and beyond them lived the nomadic Eskimos. But these lands held little appeal for settlers and little interest for government.

In 1876 fighting broke out between the American Sioux and the United States Army, and Ottawa began to hasten the treaty-making process. On 18 August 1876, the Cree and Assiniboine met with the commissioners appointed to negotiate Treaty number 6. Scarlet-coated Mounties attended to impress the Indians, and thwart any attempts to disrupt the ceremonies.

The Blackfoot came together in September 1877 at Blackfoot Crossing on the Bow River, a traditional camping and burial place of their people. Crowfoot, their

Above: Gaining the respect and confidence of the Canadian Plains Indians was a key task for the members of the fledgling Force in its early days. A pipe-smoking NWMP sergeant relaxes with his dog Indian-style with a group of Blackfoot Indians at Fort Calgary in 1876.
Opposite: Commissioner James F Macleod was Assistant Commissioner in 1876 when the NWMP's second commanding officer, George A French, resigned to rejoin the Royal Artillery. Macleod is seen here with his hand on his horse's saddle – Fort Walsh, 1878.

Above: Fort Walsh in 1876 with its log walls and buildings.
Opposite: The great Sioux chief, Sitting Bull.
Pages 34-35: Two months after leaving Dufferin, Manitoba, on 12 September 1874 on the Great March West, the travel-worn NWMP cavalcade arrived at the junction of the Bow and Belly Rivers in the land of the Blackfoot.

chief, selected the site, and to it came Lieutenant Governor Laird of the Northwest Territories, Commissioner Macleod and 100 Mounties with two nine-pounder guns.

The Blackfoot riders came 'naked except for breechcloths [and] painted in the most hideous colours from head to foot' according to a Mountie witness. They showed their prowess in horsemanship, shouting shrill war cries. Then they fought a sham battle with their traditional enemies the Crees, taking imaginary scalps, unhorsing each other and firing ball cartridges. The Blackfoot side, with the most 'scalps' to their credit, emerged as victors over the 'Cree.'

On 22 September, 70 Mounties on their horses made a passageway for the Indian chiefs and head men as they strode to the council tent. Here they made speeches, and Jerry Potts translated their words in his usual terse fashion. Crowfoot spoke first, saying briefly that the police were his friends, that their advice had been good, and that his people were thankful for their presence. He would sign the treaty with the Great White Mother and keep it as long as the sun shone and water ran. Chief Old Sun of the North Blackfoot signed next. He said that Crowfoot had spoken well, but his people wanted money, cattle and goods. Then the chiefs of the Sarcees, the North Bloods, and the Peigans signed.

At the end of the signing a nine-pounder fired a salute, and the Mountie band struck up 'The Maple Leaf Forever.' Crowfoot lit a stone pipe, took one puff, and handed it to Lieutenant Governor Laird.

Thus ended the ceremony – and a whole way of life.

In 1877, the Blackfoot, now well-off again, presented the Force with a bear skin robe showing the location of all the tribes. On it, Mounties captured whisky traders selling liquor to drunken Indians while the Great White Mother looks on approvingly. In the same year, the Mounties at Fort Macleod arrested a wealthy American whisky trader named Weatherwax, seizing his outfit and several hundred buffalo robes. The man, found guilty, fined $400 and sent to jail for six months, had everything confiscated. He shouted; 'Hold your horses there. When the wires get a-humming between Uncle Sam and Queen Vic there will be war sure.' The Mounties ignored his feeble threat.

The Mounties kept the peace between Indian tribes by swift and courageous action. In May 1877, a Saulteaux chief claimed that American Assiniboines under war leader Crow's Dance had claimed dominion over his territory and his people. Superintendent Walsh, another officer, 15 men and a scout rode out within an hour of hearing of the offence. Reaching the Assiniboine camp in the early hours, while the Indians were asleep, Walsh left four men behind to build a barricade of stones on a small hill, and rode towards the tepees. The Mounties located Crow's Dance's lodge, dragged the war leader and 19 other Indians out, and hustled back to the barricade. There they sat down to breakfast. Walsh sent a message to the Assiniboines telling them he would meet their chiefs. He lectured them about letting their warriors terrorize the Saulteaux, then took 13 Indians back to Fort Walsh for trial. Crow's Dance received six months' imprisonment at hard labour, another warrior two months and the rest were released with a warning.

Walsh became a legend in the West, a flamboyant man who gained the respect of the Indians by his direct and fearless actions. He had shown his mettle in 1876 by entering the Sioux camp of Black Moon with 12 men, and confronting the chief and his 2000 followers. Black Moon told the Mountie that he was tired of being hunted in his own country, and had crossed the border to live in peace in the land of the Great White Mother. Walsh explained this lady's laws, and warned the Indians against raiding into the United States.

Over the next few months, other Sioux arrived in Canada. The condition of some saddened Walsh who noted that 'Their warriors were silent and solemn . . . war had made the children forget how to play.'

Late in May 1877, Sitting Bull and his people moved into Canada and settled about 60 miles south-east of Fort Walsh. These were the warriors who had wiped out Custer's force at the Battle of the Little Big Horn in June 1876. Walsh rode fearlessly into their camp, and laid down the law. Sitting Bull said, 'I have buried my weapons.' Irvine also decided to visit the Sioux. Before he left the fort, six Indians arrived with a message from Sitting Bull. Three Americans had entered his camp, and been made prisoner. What should he do?

As they rode into the camp, the Indians, 'a long line of tremendously big men,' emerged from their lodges. They shook hands with the Mounties with 'a powerful grip and some nearly pulled me off my horse,' reported Walsh. Sitting Bull impressed Walsh: 'When he smiled, which he often did, his face brightened up wonderfully . . . He believes no one from [the United States] . . . and said so. His speech showed him to be a man of wonderful capability.'

Walsh and Irvine convinced Sitting Bull that he was safe in Canada, as long as he obeyed the laws. 'You and your

Horse troops of the North West Mounted Police Troop at Fort Walsh – on parade in 1878.

families can sleep sound,' said Irvine. The three American prisoners were released and the Mounties spent the night in the Sioux camp.

Walsh became known as 'Sitting Bull's Chief,' but the pressures built up from Ottawa to remove the Sioux from Canadian territory. These Indians still wore uniforms of the US Cavalry, carried the guns of the dead troopers, and wore their scalps in their belts. As the Sioux realized they were safe in Canada, others joined them until 5600 had settled near Fort Walsh. The American government set up a commission to meet with the exiled chiefs and convince them to return south. In October, Commissioner Macleod rode to the border with a troop of Mounted Policemen 'whose red uniforms and the red and white pennons affixed to their lances contrasted beautifully with the monotonous dun colour of the plains around them,' according to the *New York Herald*. Here they met General Terry, leader of the American commission – who had led the campaign that had driven the Sioux into Canada.

Above: The North West Mounted Police Band at Fort Walsh, 1878. It was a brass band with drums.
Right: Another North West Mounted Police outpost – Fort Macleod in 1879 – named for Commissioner James F Macleod, who had been put in command two years before.

Sitting Bull and the other chiefs met the American delegation at Fort Walsh. They showed their friendship with the Mounties by shaking hands with Macleod and Walsh. Sitting Bull told the Americans that he and his people had found peace in Canada. He rejected their terms for returning to the United States, then allowed a woman to address the council – a calculated insult.

The American Sioux settled in their Canadian sanctuary, but continued to steal horses – including some belonging to the Mounties. When Sub-Inspector Allen rode to the Sioux camp, he found Sitting Bull on a fine horse. The chief told him that the police would not get their horses back. Allen said he would take Sitting Bull's horse if he thought it stolen. The Indian calmly replied that it was, whereupon the officer moved his horse closer to that of Sitting Bull, lifted him from the saddle, and pulled the horse from under him. Then the police party rode back to the fort.

The starvation years forced the Sioux south over the next few years. In 1877, export tax was paid on 30,000 buffalo robes at Fort Macleod; two years later the figure had fallen to 5764. Indians accustomed to a feast or famine existence began to suffer from continual hunger, and Canadian Indians blamed the disappearance of the buffalo on the American Sioux. A mild winter in 1877-78 brought a light snowfall, and in the spring the prairie fires drove the buffalo north, and south into the United States. By the summer of 1879, no game remained on the prairies, and Indians were eating mice, grass, their dogs and even their horses. The police posts, besieged by starving Indians, shared their rations with people who 'looked like a delegation from some graveyard.' In 1880-81, smallpox swept through the Qu'Appelle district and Constable Holmes risked his life and travelled hard for hundreds of miles to vaccinate Indians, Métis and Whites.

Macleod wrote to Ottawa that he thought it 'a wonderful thing how well the Indian has behaved under all the circumstances.' Walsh noted 'their strict observance of the law and order would reflect credit upon the most civilised community.'

In November 1879, the first murder of a Mountie took place. Constable Marmaduke Graburn had been in the Force for six months, and had turned back to recover an axe after a spell of herd duty outside Fort Walsh. When he failed to return, Jerry Potts led a search party over the snow-covered land, found the body, but lost the tracks of the killers. Two Indians claimed that a Blood named Star Child had killed Graburn. Corporal Patterson made a spectacular arrest in an Indian camp, disarming Star Child, and carrying him away under his arm while other Indians tried to rescue him. At the Indian's trial in October 1881, the six-man settler jury returned a verdict of not guilty, apparently afraid of triggering an Indian war or a raid on their stock.

The first execution of an Indian took place a few days before Christmas, 1879. In the spring of the year, a well-built Cree named Swift Runner had been arrested at Fort Saskatchewan. In a time of starvation he looked far too well fed, and the police uncovered the reason. He had eaten his mother, brother, wife and five children.

By 1880 the buffalo had vanished, the Sioux were making nuisances of themselves by killing cattle, and the power of Sitting Bull had waned. Ottawa felt that Walsh was encouraging the Indian chief to remain in Canada. They moved him from Fort Walsh, replacing him with Superintendent Crozier who wasted no time in urging the Sioux to accept the American terms for resettlement. They began to trickle back over the border, but Sitting Bull held out to the last.

After a starvation winter, he led 200 of his people south and surrendered to the military authorities at Fort Buford, Montana, in July 1881.

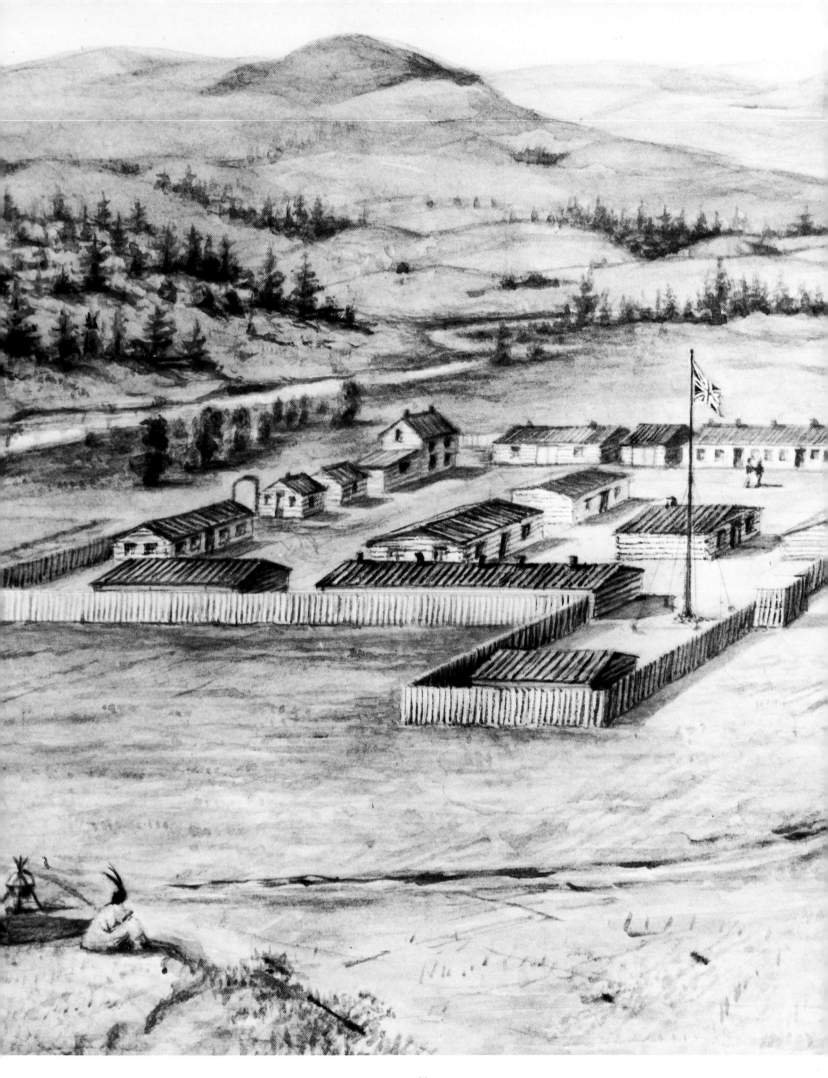

Chapter 5

'THE MOUNTED POLICE DON'T SCARE WORTH A CENT.'

Americans soon came to admire the Mounties' style. The Fort Benton (Montana) *Record* claimed that 'The Mounted Police don't scare worth a cent.'

The Sioux departed, the Canadian Indians moved to reserves, and the whisky trade declined. So the NWMP concentrated its attention on horse stealing. In 1882, Commissioner Irvine reported that the Cypress Hills were 'infested with horse thieves.' The Force rounded up and returned stolen horses to the United States, but the Americans did not reciprocate. The NWMP recovered horses stolen by Canadian Indians from settlers, and mediated between Bloods and Crees. The Mounties recovered Cree horses from the Bloods, overlooking a minor skirmish outside Fort Walsh in which a Cree, described by Irvine as 'an idiot and almost blind,' was killed and scalped.

Only 38 cases came before the magistrates at Fort Walsh in 1882. Fourteen dealt with liquor, and two with horse stealing. Ka-ke-ew went to penitentiary for two years at hard labour for horse stealing. Jean Baptiste Robillard received three years for the same offence on 26 June, but escaped from the guard room and remained at large at the end of the year.

Irvine's report for this year also included a letter from W C VanHorne, General Manager of the Canadian Pacific Railway, acknowledging his obligations to the Mounted Police, 'whose zeal and industry in preventing the traffic in liquor and preserving order along the line under

Above: A photograph of North West Mounted Policemen and their prisoners taken in the prison yard of Regina Prison during the trial after the North West Rebellion in 1875.
Opposite: A sketch of the wooden walls and buildings of Fort Walsh. This was the headquarters of the North West Mounted Police from 1878 until 1882.

Above: A photograph of the North West Mounted Police detachment at Fort Carlton – 1884-85.
Opposite: Chief Poundmaker, an ally of Louis Riel.

construction have contributed so much to the successful prosecution of the work.'

The government contract with the railway gave it a grant of 25 million acres 'fairly fit for settlement' and the Indians and the Métis soon recognized what its presence meant for their way of life. Cree under Piapot, self-styled 'Lord of Heaven and Earth,' pitched their camp on the right of-way. Corporal Wilde pulled out his watch and gave the Indians 15 minutes to move. Then he dismounted, kicked down the centre pole of Piapot's tent, and did the same to the other lodges. The Indians moved, and the track laying went on.

The Commissioner reported in 1883 that 'the Indians were so kept in subjection that no opposition of any moment [to the railway] was encountered from them.'

The Force had also to keep order among thousands of rough navvies who built the railway, suppress the whisky trade among them, and guard the trains and the track during strikes. Some 'malcontents' at Moose Jaw, thwarted in their efforts to damage railway engines, tried to poison the local water with alkali, acid and red pepper.

The Mounties also handled numerous cases concerning non-payment of wages by sub-contractors. As the railway

pushed through the Rockies, Sam Steele and eight Mounties protected workers from moonshiners, gamblers and toughs, stopped the sale of liquor within 20 miles of the track and intervened in strikes. When work crews struck on 1 April 1885, Steele pleaded with them to be patient. Violence broke out when strikers tried to stop workers laying track, and the Mounties arrested the ringleader. As they neared the post, the mob rushed them. Steele had been sick in bed with fever. He leapt up, grabbed a Winchester, and rushed out of the post, shouting 'Halt or I'll fire.' The mob halted and the prisoner was hustled into a cell.

On the prairies, the Métis took up arms in 1885 to halt the changes threatening their way of life. Living on riverside farms, these people traded and carried goods across the prairies, linking Indians and whites, and sharing some of the characteristics of each group. Describing themselves as 'free and spirited' men, they resented the incursions of central Canadian merchants and speculators. In 1870, under Louis Riel, an intelligent, charismatic leader, the Métis created a provisional government that moved into the vacuum created by the waning of the Hudson's Bay Company's power.

Macdonald sent British redcoats and Canadian militia to keep the peace, brought Manitoba into being to provide for representative government, and allowed Riel to go into exile.

In 1884, the Métis called back their leader, who met with Indian chiefs and sought their support. The Mounties, he claimed, would be 'wiped out of existence' within a week. On 18 March 1885, the rebels cut the telegraph wires at Batoche, their headquarters south of Prince Albert in the Saskatchewan river country. Irvine marched from Regina to Prince Albert through deep snow and bitter cold, with every available man. Crozier put Battleford on a war footing, then headed for Fort Carlton. With 55 police, 43 Prince Albert Volunteers and a seven-pounder gun he rode straight into an ambush at Duck Lake where Métis and Indians under Gabriel Dumont, the gifted guerilla leader, poured fire into the column. Crozier pulled back after losing nine volunteers and one policeman; two Mounties died of wounds later. The other side lost five killed.

Indians then attacked Frog Lake Catholic Mission, 35 miles north of Fort Pitt where Inspector Dickens commanded a detachment. After looting the Hudson's Bay store, they took the white prisoners to their camp, and killed seven of them, including two Catholic priests. On 13 April, Big Bear and 250 mounted Cree demanded the surrender of the police. The Indian chief also asked for tea and tobacco, and a blanket as he was 'very cold.' The goods were sent, the surrender demand rejected.

Dickens, 'so confused and excited he did not know what to suggest, nor how to act,' according to one of the besieged, agreed to let the civilians go to the Indian camp. Then he abandoned Fort Pitt which the Indians looted as Chickenstalker and his men crawled down the North Saskatchewan to Battleford in leaky boats.

Ottawa sent 5000 militia under Major-General Middleton, a blimpish British soldier, to crush the uprising. He referred to the Mounties as 'gophers' who had ducked into their holes when danger threatened. Sam Steele recruited 25 Mounties, 100 cowboys and settlers, John McDougall the missionary and four Stoney Indians who scouted and skirmished as Middleton's column plodded towards Batoche and overwhelmed the rebels in a final battle.

Riel surrendered on 15 May, was tried and condemned to hang. He spent his last days guarded by the NWMP in Regina. Constable Donkin found him 'always most studiously polite and painfully deferential.' On 16 November 1885, Donkin and three other Mounties, half asleep, their feet chilled, rode out of Regina at four in the morning, into a magnificent sunrise, to check the passes of those who had come to see Riel die. Commissioner Irvine stood on the platform at that moment.

Big Bear had surrendered on 2 July 1885, and gone to Stony Mountain Penitentiary north of Winnipeg; he received amnesty in the following year.

Discontent continued to simmer among the Indians as Blackfoot and Cree gave their last war cries. Seven Blackfoot threatened to burn down a lumber mill in the Cypress Hills in the summer of 1885. By the time the Mounties reached their camp, they had disappeared. Superintendent McIllree asked the Indians to produce the men 'but with no avail.' He wrote that if the accused men had been found 'we should have had to fight for their capture, which I was prepared to do, but which I am thankful to say did not happen.' He added that 'the Indians told me that they did not know who we were, being in brown suits.'

From Prince Albert, Superintendent Perry reported of the year after the rebellion that he had 'not received a complaint by any person against an Indian, nor have I heard of them threatening or troubling settlers. Oftimes hungry, poorly clad and suffering, still they have not helped themselves, but applied to the Indian Department for succor, which is usually liberally granted . . . The half-breed population . . . would appear to have forgotten the late troubles . . . They were assisted largely by freighting the lumber for the police barracks at Battleford.'

In British Columbia, the Indians of the inaccessible Kootenay District refused to live on reserves. Under Chief Isadore they raided a jail, and released two of their number held in connection with the murder of two miners. Sam Steele took two officers and 75 men to the Kootenays in 1887 and built Fort Steele. Chief Isadore and the men he had liberated appeared before Steele, and were acquitted; the Mountie found himself 'pleased with the bearing of the Indians . . . They showed great intelligence, and it was clear that they knew nothing of the murder.' During their 12 months in the area, not one case of theft or drunkenness came before the Mounties. But four of them died of typhoid.

In the last decade of the century, four Indians died violently as a way of life vanished. And four Mounties died trying to bring them to justice.

The Almighty Voice incident has generated a whole set of mythologies. This Cree Indian is alleged to have asked the Indian agent at Duck Lake for beef to make broth for a sick child, and been refused. He was arrested by the Mounties after killing a government animal, and taken to Duck Lake post where a Mountie, the myth goes, told him that he would hang for his crime. Since the detachment had no jail, Almight Voice slept on the floor and he escaped when the guard fell asleep.

Sergeant Colebrook and a Métis scout from Batoche caught up with Almighty Voice who shouted a warning in Cree, then shot Colebrook. The Indian avoided capture for over a year, then wounded a scout at Duck Lake. The Mounties and civilians at Prince Albert, holding a smoking concert after a cricket match, saddled up and set off in pursuit of the Indian as soon as they heard the news. They found the fugitive and two companions dug in on a bluff. An inspector and a sergeant were wounded while searching for them. Corporal Hockin, left in charge, decided to charge the bluff. A Mountie and the postmaster

Opposite: **A photograph of Louis Riel taken by a New York State photographer, A J Owen of Reeseville, while Riel was in hiding.** *Pages 46-47:* **An unhorsed rider in a buffalo hunt.**

Above: The camp of 'D' Troop of the North West Mounted Police in the Kootenay Pass, British Columbia, 1888.
Far left: A steam ferry transporting Canadian soldiers across the South Saskatchewan River during the North West Rebellion in 1885.
Left: A photo taken at Fort Pitt in 1884 during the North West Rebellion. Chief Big Bear and his sons.
Below: A scene of militia camp life during the North West Rebellion – 1885.

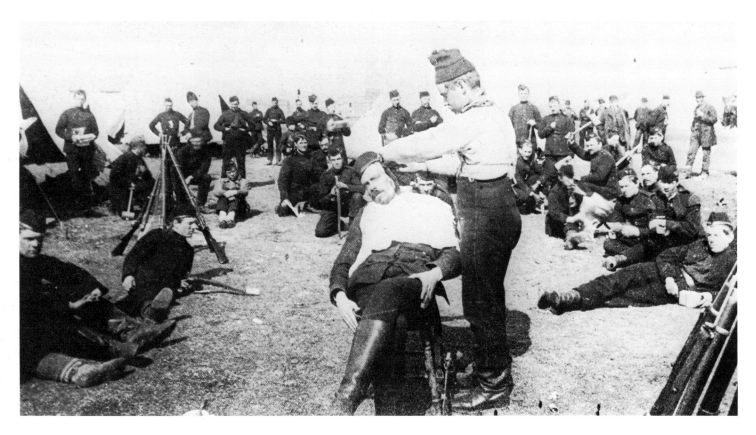

at Duck Lake died in the attack. Hockin, wounded in the attack, died later.

Reinforcements arrived with a nine-pounder gun. Almighty Voice called out that he was a brave man, and ready for another fight. The Mounties picked off one of his companions, and on 28 May 1897, shelled the bluff for half an hour. Then they charged. But Almighty Voice and his companion lay dead in their rifle pit.

In the previous year, Sergeant Wilde, who had confronted and cowed Piapot, left the Pincher Creek detachment to arrest Charcoal, a Blood who had killed another Indian. On 11 November 1896, the Mountie caught up with the killer in bitter weather, his rifle across the saddle as a sign of peace. Charcoal shot Wilde, knocking him from his horse, then put another bullet into his stomach. Then he rode to the home of his brothers who turned him over to the police.

Charcoal died on the gallows on 16 March 1897. He had lost the use of his legs, and went to his death tied to a chair.

The Blood had terrified Red Crow, a chief. When Steele had visited this Indian's home in 1895, he found it 'very comfortable,' with carpets, white sheets on the beds and clean windows. It compared 'favourably with the residence of the average settler,' noted Steele.

Right: Another scene of militia camp life during the North West Rebellion – 1885. Some troops are in formation, some are resting and one man is getting a haircut.
Below: Mounties on duty at the end of the Canadian Pacific Railway tracks at Golden, British Columbia, 1886.

Chapter 6

REORGANIZING THE FORCE

Sir John A Macdonald's Conservatives had fallen from power by the time the Force marched west. Once in opposition they wasted no time attacking the government for the organizational problems of the new body.

To their voices was added that of Commissioner French who complained continually about the location of Swan River as the Force's headquarters. Remote from both Ottawa and Blackfoot country, the post had been designed by architects who knew little about life in the west. Strung out in a line a thousand feet long, the barracks sat atop a treeless, boulder-strewn hill infested with snakes; the Mounties celebrated Queen Victoria's birthday on 24 May 1875, by killing 1100 reptiles. By this time their scarlet jackets had rotted away, and the men dressed in collections of rags or deerskins. A monotonous diet of buffalo meat, pork, beans, flapjacks and tea compounded the boredom of police life on the prairies. The barracks lacked toilets, a kitchen, a washroom, a guard room and roofs for the stables, and the wind whistled through holes in walls built of green lumber. Some Mounties had not been paid for months and fell into debt with the traders who settled around the police posts. French recommended that a band be formed at Swan River. The members had to pay for their own instruments, and to have them shipped by dog team from Winnipeg. Men began to desert. Assistant Commissioner Macleod left the force to become a magistrate, and Inspector Carvell, a former Confederate officer, went on holiday in the United States and sent in his resignation.

Above: James F Macleod, who was commissioner of the North West Mounted Police from 22 July 1876 to 31 October 1880.
Opposite: A photograph of the members of the North West Mounted Police Detachment at Fort Steele, British Columbia, taken in August 1888.

Captain John French of the North West Mounted Police.

Minor mutinies marked the early years of the Force. At Fort Macleod, the Assistant Commissioner dealt with one 'buck' by going from barrack to barrack to discuss the men's problems, reducing one malcontent in rank, and giving another a tongue-lashing.

Newspapers in Toronto and Winnipeg joined the Opposition in criticizing the conditions under which the Force served. In 1875, Liberal Prime Minister Alexander Mackenzie sent Major-General Edward Selby, head of the Canadian Militia, to enquire about conditions in the NWMP. The constables impressed Selby with their 'willingness, endurance, and, as far as I can learn, integrity and character,' but he found that some inspectors fell short of 'power, ability or attainments.' He concluded that 'for a newly-raised force, hastily enrolled and equipped, it is in very fair order' and that 'Too much value cannot be attached to the North West Mounted Police, too much attention cannot be paid to their efficiency.'

Commissioner French's constant demand for better conditions for his men resulted in his dismissal by Order-in-Council on 22 July 1876. When he left Swan River, the NCOs presented him with an address and a gold watch. He shook hands with everyone, looking 'very sad' according to an eyewitness. French went on to become a major general in the British Army and was knighted before his death in 1921.

James Farquharson Macleod took his place as Commissioner. Born in Scotland, trained as a lawyer, Macleod served in the militia during the Red River Rebellion of 1870. A tough, charming man and a hard drinker, Macleod wore a heavy beard and curling moustaches. He moved the Force's headquarters from Swan River to Fort Macleod. While stamping out the whisky trade, the Mounties did not neglect their own need for liquid refreshment. A trader at Fort Macleod ordered three gallons of the best whisky from Fort Shaw, Montana, instructing that it be sent to Inspector Crozier with the bill and adding 'he is all right on the pay.' At Wood Mountain the men drank Florida water, cologne, pain-killer, bay rum and even mustang liniment.

In the summers the Mounties suffered from 'mountain fever,' a form of typhoid caused by dead animals in the water supply and the careless habits of the settlers in disposing of their garbage. In the winter came colds, coughs, rheumatism and throat infections as the men tried to keep warm in barracks where snow piled up on the floors. A sub-constable at Swan River froze his ears when he left them exposed during the night.

When Macdonald's Conservatives returned to power in 1878, they simplified the system of ranks and titles, and also cut the rates of pay which fell to 40 cents a day on enrolment. Constables who re-engaged saw their pay drop from 75 to 50 cents a day, and those who retired no longer received land grants. In 1880, Macdonald appointed Fred White, his former secretary, as Comptroller of the NWMP. White, a bureaucrat's bureaucrat, retained the position until 1912. He insulated the Commissioner from direct political influence while explaining the Mounties' activities to eastern politicians who had only the vaguest notion of conditions out west. He told them that it cost half as much to maintain a Mountie as it did to sustain a US Cavalry trooper. Macdonald wanted to enroll native peoples in the Force. White rejected the idea, conjuring up visions of Indians and Métis and their families swarming around police posts—'a source of much inconvenience and anxiety.'

In the year that White assumed his position, Macleod left his. He had been serving as a magistrate as well as running the Force, and the burden of the two duties became too much for this 'gentleman of the old school and . . . man of the world and affairs.' The parsimonious Sir John A nagged him constantly about the Force's expenditure which he claimed 'would not stand investigation.'

Acheson Gosford Irvine, the Force's first Canadian-born Commissioner, also described as 'a thorough gentleman,' served for six years. Nicknamed 'Old Sorrel Top,' Irvine proved too kind and good-natured to wield authority effectively. And as the threat of Indian uprisings diminished, the settlers began to see disadvantages in an energetic and incorruptible police force. South of the border, communities elected their law officers who were thus subject to local control. In Canada, admiration for the Mounties became mixed with resentment about some of their activities, especially those related to preventing

Acheson Gosford Irvine, who was Commissioner of the North West Mounted Police from 1 November 1880 to 31 March 1886.

The North West Mounted Police Association soccer team of 1896.

pioneers from easing the pains of their solitary life with alcohol.

An ordinance of 1875 prohibited the import of liquor into the Northwest Territories, save for medicinal and sacramental purposes. Seven years later, the thirst of Westerners was eased a little when the Lieutenant-Governor began to issue individual permits for liquor. This widely-abused system made it even more difficult to stop the flow of liquor into the Territories. The police had to check permits while smuggled liquor flowed into the West in hollowed-out Bibles, eggs, barrels of oatmeal, canned apples and coffins. In 1880, Constable William Parker, a clergyman's son, arrested a man who lacked a liquor permit. He had carried freight from Winnipeg to Qu'Appelle for the police, and presented them with a bottle of liquor as a token of appreciation. Parker pounced on him, and the man was fined $50 and $11 costs. Parker wrote to his father: '. . . he paid the fine & I received half of it and one dollar & a half of the costs. Paying business for me, eh? The prosecutor in such cases always gets half the fine.'

Most of the Mounties found enforcing the liquor ordinance 'a most disagreeable duty' as one officer put it. Informers were hard to find, local magistrates dismissed cases on the flimsiest pretext and western lawyers soon found loopholes in the law.

And the members of the Force did not present a good example, being also prone to seeking solace in strong drink. In Battleford in 1882, several NCOs drank ether, and as their commanding officer reported, 'The effect was most disastrous. Sergeant Waltham for a time being was a regular lunatic.' At Fort Macleod, two drunken policemen held up a traveller at gunpoint to obtain money for drink. At another post, a bugler staggered from his barracks, blew a few notes of 'The Last Post' and passed out cold on the parade square. For this he received a $10 fine and three months at hard labour.

The officers encouraged sports, games and celebrations to relieve the monotony of life on the prairies. William Parker played football in a foot of snow at ten below zero on Christmas Day, 1882. He did not want to play, but not because of the weather. His commanding officer ordered him to do so, and Parker wrote, 'As I expected, the civilians made a dead set against me, tore my shirt clean off, kicked me in the nose until the blood was flowing freely . . . But we had the satisfaction of winning the game.'

Parker obviously loved the life of a Mountie. He wrote of the prairie 'white with geese' and of the joys of hunting. He learned how to build smudge fires to keep away mosquitoes, to bake bread with a buffalo chip fire, and to avoid snowblindness by blackening his eyelids with charcoal. Parched for a drink, he took the advice of an Indian and drank blood-streaked milk from the udder of a dead buffalo cow. When an officer rode up, Parker invited him to stop for a drink. The officer shouted back, 'I always thought you were a beast. And now I know it.'

The Mounties brought a new value to the Canadian West, based on the eastern concept of the Indian as a noble savage, and not as a murderous brute. Sophisticated and disciplined, the officers and many of their men did not share the egalitarian and individualistic ways of the American West or of the settlers who trickled into the prairies as life became safe there. One Mountie wrote: 'The prairie was carpeted with wild roses, and for a time I tried to avoid stepping on them, but they were so plentiful that the avoidance of them became irksome and I hardened my heart and walked on.'

Such sensitivities did not stop the Mounties from following orders and doing their duty.

Parker once carried urgent mail from Shoal River to Swan River, travelling 140 miles in 26 hours, without sleep, swimming the Assiniboine River on the way. He

Left: This photograph is thought to be the first North West Mounted Police Banff Detachment.
Opposite: L W Herchmer, the North West Mounted Police Commissioner from 1 April 1886 to 31 July 1900.
Opposite inset: A sergeant in the North West Mounted Police dress uniform of 1885.

drove a buckboard and a single horse, and after 100 miles, his dog Spot 'could run no further and had to be left behind.' When a wheel of the buckboard broke, Parker cached the heavy mail and rode the rest of the way bareback on the horse. In 1889, Parker and three other Mounties strode into an Indian camp to arrest a man who said he would not be taken alive. They had trouble finding the right Indian, and his companions became hostile as they hustled him away. 'I fully expected to get a bullet in my back any minute,' wrote Parker. The chief and 50 armed Indians rode after them, demanding the release of the prisoner. The leader of the patrol refused, and it returned to Qu'Appelle after travelling 100 miles in 24 hours.

Parker also had entrepreneurial instincts, and augmented his meagre pay by contracting with the Force to cut timber and hay, raising and selling potatoes, and buying land in Winnipeg for speculation. As sole representatives of the central government, the Mounties undertook a wide range of official tasks – and a few unofficial ones. A letter in the Manitoba *Daily Free Press* of 19 September 1883 crystallized the discontents of the settlers with the force:

> It is about time that officers in this outfit confined themselves exclusively to their duties as such, and left the management of horse and cattle ranches, coal mines, ferry boats, bogus horse sales, chasing half-breeds all over the Northwest with Government horses after land script, to those who are not fortunate enough to hold commissions in this force.

In the previous year, Commissioner Irvine had pointed out to Ottawa the difficulties of policing 375,000 square miles of the Northwest Territories with only 300 men. The Force added 200 recruits who arrived in 1883 at the 'great muddy expanse' in Regina selected as the headquarters and training depot for the Force.

Inspector Richard Deane, a former Royal Marine officer, also arrived in Regina in the same year, and found that the NWMP had existed for ten years 'without a single standing order or regulation of any kind.' He described his companions as 'an armed mob.' During the first 18 years of its existence, the Force became the responsibility of seven different ministers, including the one for Railways and Canals.

Irvine did what he could to improve conditions, but he had trouble sorting out trivial matters from crucial ones. He suggested a new design for the cap, and complained continually about the lack of bedsteads for the men. Meanwhile the rank and file usually suffered in silence, but some staged bucks.

After early morning patrol on the day that Riel died, Constable Donkin's troop did not return to breakfast as they'd hoped. Instead 'we were ordered to fall in . . . and kept marching and counter-marching to suit the whims of some one who was muddle headed enough to imagine it was of use.' Donkin wrote of the 'wear and tear and the constant irritations' of life in the Force, adding that

Right: A band of Indians with their wagons and horses entering Fort Macleod in 1891. The log buildings have given way to buildings made out of boards.

'nowhere is the gilt so ruthlessly stripped from the gingerbread as in the North West.'

At Edmonton the men refused to carry out orders in 1886 because of filthy living conditions and unsatisfactory promotion procedures. Mounties from Regina arrested the ringleaders who went to prison before being dismissed from the Force. The decline of discipline and the poor showing in the 1885 uprising led to Irvine's retirement a year after the Duck Lake fiasco. He had suggested many reforms, but lacked the will and the political power to implement them. Lawrence Herchmer, his successor, had both. A friend of Sir John A, the new Commissioner, son of a clergyman, had served in the British Army and worked on the commission that established the US-Canadian boundary before founding and running a brewery in Winnipeg. A brusque, irascible man, Herchmer appointed his brother Assistant Commissioner as a first step. In 1889 he issued 'Regulations and Orders' for running the Force. New buildings replaced the crude log structures at many posts, and a proper riding school was built at Regina. Food and living accommodations were improved, recreation rooms and non-profit canteens set up, 4% beer made available in the barracks, and a pension plan introduced for NCOs and constables.

Herchmer cracked down on drinking and irregular activities.

A drunken officer at Maple Creek was given the choice of resigning or being dismissed; he resigned. When another officer posted a constable, the man complained that he would lose heavily on some pigs he'd purchased. Herchmer wrote acidly to the officer, 'How did he manage those pigs on patrol?'

Herchmer had introduced the patrol system shortly after being appointed. The Mounties travelled one and a half million miles a year on horseback to oversee 'the movement of doubtful characters, conditions of crops, prospects of hay, the ownership of any particular fine horses.' They made themselves known to every settler. By 1891, the land between Manitoba and British Columbia contained about 90,000 inhabitants, including Indians and Métis. Over the next 25 years, a million settlers would move into this land. Police patrols along the American border prevented horse and cattle rustling, and other Mounties covered those parts of the prairies where no regular trails existed. The telephone and the telegraph extended the reach of the police, and the Force began using typewriters before they came into general use in government.

The Commissioner reported in 1887 that 422 cases, including seven murders, had been 'disposed of in the North-West Territories.' About a third of the cases concerned liquor, but the Force had also to deal with someone who shot a hen and 11 'dangerous lunatics.'

Herchmer's excessive zeal and abrupt manner led to a government enquiry into his rule in 1891. None of the charges against the Commissioner held up, but the investigating judge found that he had acted in an overbearing manner and misunderstood his authority.

In 1885, the Force numbered just over 1000 officers and men, many of them hastily recruited on the outbreak of the troubles. With the 'remarkable absence of crime' its numbers dwindled to around 750 when a new Commissioner, A B Perry, took office. Herchmer had gone to war in South Africa, and the government used his absence to get rid of this difficult man.

When Perry took over he thought he would have to preside over the dissolution of the NWMP.

By 1900, the Mounties had added to their legendary status by bringing law and order to a new frontier in the Yukon during the Klondike Gold Rush. And, as the flood of settlers moved into the 'last, best West,' they stood ready to meet new challenges.

Chapter 7

THE FORCE IN THE YUKON

In 1852, coastal Indians descended the Yukon River and burned out the Hudson's Bay Company post at Fort Selkirk, upriver from the site of Dawson. On a journey down the Yukon 30 years later, Lieutenant Frederick Schwatka of the United States Army did not see a single Indian – 'and only one deserted house, with an occasional peeled pole at long intervals that marked the temporary camp of the few wandering Indians.' At that time, the boundary between Canada and the United States in what became the Yukon Territory was very vague. In 1887, Leroy Napoleon McQuesten and Arthur Harper built their trading post at the mouth of the Fortymile River where it joined the Yukon, a few miles upstream from where they guessed the Alaska boundary lay. Fortymile soon became the centre of settlement in the unorganized territory, and over the winter of 1892-93, 210 miners waited here for spring breakup. They enforced the law through miners' meetings.

In 1893, John J Healey, builder of Fort Whoop-Up, ran afoul of this method of meting out justice. The miners disliked Healey's habit of billing them monthly and demanding prompt payment. When he laid a complaint about a servant before a meeting, the miners found in favour of the girl and fined Healey heavily. The trader wrote to Sam Steele demanding an end to this kind of community rule. Anglican Bishop Bompas had already become concerned over the way in which the Indians followed the example of the miners 'in irreligion and

Above: A sergeant of the North West Mounted Police in his dress uniform – 1898.
Opposite: A photograph of the Town Station Detachment in Dawson, Yukon Territory in 1897.

debauchery.' Bompas' letters to Ottawa nudged the government towards action in the unpoliced north. William Ogilvie, a government surveyor, visited the Territory in 1893 and told the Minister of the Interior that the miners and traders he met chafed under the restrictions of the Yukon mining law. Such people might just encourage an American take-over of the area, especially if someone made a big strike.

And so Inspector Charles Constantine, the Force's trouble shooter, son of an Anglican clergyman, went north on a fact-finding mission, with Staff Sergeant Charles Brown, a skilled boatman. The Mounties reached Fortymile on 7 August 1894, and Constantine spent a month there, obtaining first-hand information on the country. Then he headed south to write his report, leaving Brown to winter over at Fortymile.

Constantine described the community as 'very quiet' except when the miners arrived to winter over and 'there is

Left: Surrounded by piles of supplies for Yukon Gold Rush miners and prospectors, NWMP members man the Chilcoot Pass customs posts on the Canada-US border in 1897.
Below: Things were busy during the Gold Rush – a place called Profanity Hill – 1896-97.
Opposite: Left to right: Superintendant S B Steele (North West Mounted Police), Miss Scott, Inspector C Starnes (NWMP) and Mrs Starnes. Captain Burstall (Yukon Field Force), later Sir Henry Burstall, Chief of General Staff National Defence, Dawson, Yukon Territory, 1899.

a general carouse accompanied with the firing of pistols and guns.' There had been only one shooting and cutting case over the last winter, and both parties had been drunk. Women were treated with respect by the miners, who spent most of the winter gambling. Constantine dismissed the Indians as a 'lazy and shiftless lot.' About half the Yukon residents were Americans, and the rest Canadians. A miners' meeting had refused permission for a party of Japanese and Chinese to enter the interior. Constantine wrote:

> **The miners are very jealous of what they consider their rights, and from what I could see and learn, any enforcement of different laws will have to be backed up with a strong force at least for a while.**

About $300,000 in gold had been produced in 1893, and Constantine undertook the 'distasteful' task of collecting $3348.82 in customs dues. About 3000 gallons of liquor were expected to reach the Yukon in 1894, and the miners and the Indians had acquired great skills in building stills and making 'hooch.'

The inspector signed his report on 10 October 1894, and sent it off to the President of the Privy Council in Ottawa. Then he returned to duty at Moosomin in the Northwest Territories. On 1 June 1895, a group of Mounties left Regina for the Yukon, led by Constantine, who had been appointed Agent-General for the territory, as well as magistrate, gold commissioner, land agent and collector of customs. The force consisted of two officers and their wives, an assistant-surgeon, and 16 NCOs and men and it arrived at Fortymile after a 2000 mile journey up the Yukon River in early July. The Mounties cleared the land opposite the community and built Fort Constantine. Then they cut wood for the stoves as winter approached; the going price of $8 a cord was too high for the tight police budget. That winter temperatures dipped to −73°F. In his annual report, Constantine noted that only one man had been ordered to leave camp as a potential troublemaker. Only one case of selling liquor to the Indians and one of assault had come before him. Reports of a blood feud among the Indians proved later to be without foundation.

Mounties hoist the flags of Canada and the United States during the Gold Rush – White Pass Summit, 1899.

In the following year, Constantine's men improved the post, enforced the mining regulations, and found the miners a peaceful lot. Miners' meetings and frontier law disappeared as the Force asserted its authority. One wrongdoer was taken to the Yukon, placed in a canoe, given a slab of bacon and pushed off.

And then, in August 1896, two men walked through the gates of Fort Constantine to stake their claims on Rabbit Creek. Tagish Charlie and George Carmack had panned gold from this stream which flowed into a river called the Trondiuck about a mile from its mouth. Rabbit Creek became Bonanza, and the Klondike Rush started. Miners and traders abandoned Fortymile and headed for the new diggings. A settlement arose where the Klondike flowed into the Yukon – Dawson City.

And the Mounties in the Yukon suddenly became very busy. In the fall of 1896, Constantine received reinforcements and immediately sent Inspector Scarth to Dawson to build Fort Herchmer. He found chaos. Supplies were short, the American miners chafing under Canadian law, typhoid threatening to break out, and many miners were destitute and starving. Scarth rationed supplies, advised the residents to clean up the townsite, and sent many residents downriver where food was cheaper and more plentiful.

The Force adopted a strategy of controlling the rivers and the passes, and keeping an eye on everyone entering the territory. Inspector Moodie was given the task in the fall of 1897 of finding an all-Canadian route to the Klondike. With Constable F J Fitzgerald, three specials and two guides, he plunged into the trackless land northwest of Edmonton. After 14 months, innumerable hardships and incredible escapes from danger, the party reached Fort Selkirk. Moodie stated simply, 'I should say the overland route would never be used in face of the quick and easy one via Skagway.'

Alaska was a lawless land. In Skagway, the gateway to the Yukon, 'Soapy' Smith and his gang terrorized the town and fleeced the goldseekers. In 1898, Joseph Tyrrell, a government geologist, arrived in Skagway with $2000 in official funds. He enlisted the help of a 'pleasant young man' to help him find the Mountie detachment that looked after the interests of Canadians. They passed a saloon where Tyrrell, lured into throwing the dice by the young man, was told that he was entitled to half the pot when he won. Tyrrell drew back, avoiding a phoney fight over the rigged game. When he located the Mounties, the sergeant told him that the young man, 'Slim Jim' Foster, specialized in fleecing newcomers. After being robbed in the saloon, known as 'The Slaughter House,' victims ended up in the tidal waters behind it.

Early in 1898 Sam Steele headed for the Yukon. He noted that 'robbery and murder were daily occurrences' in Skagway; bullets passed through the NWMP post while he lay abed one Sunday. The Mounties established posts at the summits of the snow-blanketed Chilkoot and White Passes, and ensured that no one without a year's supply of food entered the Yukon. Steele headed for Lake Bennett where thousands of goldseekers were building boats and waiting for open water to sail them down to Dawson. Here he slept on a cot over a suitcase containing $2 million for a bank in the new community. When the ice went out on the lake, a vast armada of vessels of all shapes and sizes sailed away. Many of them came to grief on the only major obstacle to a smooth passage down river – Miles Canyon and the Whitehorse Rapids, just above the site of the present capital of the Yukon.

By the time Steele arrived at Miles Canyon, about 150 boats had been wrecked and at least five people drowned. He spoke to the crowd waiting to shoot the canyon and the rapids and laid down the law:

Many of your countrymen have said that the mounted police make up the laws as they go along. I am going to do so now for your own good.

No boat was allowed to run the rapids unless a Mountie had found it safe. Offenders were fined $100. Women and children walked around the rapids. And no more lives were lost.

On 7 July, Sam Steele, promoted to Lieutenant-Colonel and put in charge of the NWMP in the Yukon, moved its headquarters to Dawson. Police posts sprang up along the rivers to keep an eye on the goldseekers, and detachments were stationed in the rash of small mining towns around Dawson. In time, 250 Mounties kept the peace in the Yukon, which became a territory in 1898, with a measure of self-government. Steele licensed gambling houses, and ensured that the games were fair. Petty thieves, drunks and others ended up serving their sentences on the police woodpile. When Steele fined a gambler $50, he laughed and said, 'I've got that in my vest pocket.' The Mountie went on, 'And 60 days on the wood pile. Have you got that in your vest pocket?' Prostitution flourished, but the Mounties did not harass the girls. As Dawson lost its gold rush bloom and became more respectable, they moved the cribs across the river to Lousetown.

In his report on 1898, the peak year of the Klondike Rush, Sam Steele stated:

More than 30,000 persons, every one of whom received assistance and advice [from the NWMP] has passed down [the Yukon] . . . We had seen that the sick were cared for, had buried the dead . . . had built our own quarters and administered the laws of Canada without one well-founded complaint against us. Only three homicides had taken place, none of them preventable.

In the Yukon, even a casual labourer could earn more in a day than a Mounted Policeman could in a week. A few Mounties succumbed to temptation and went to prison. But William Ogilvie simply stated 'what everyone in this territory knows' when he wrote that the police had performed their duties in the 'highest possible manner and with the greatest efficiency.'

When Steele left the Yukon in 1899, he was surprised to see many thousands of people had come to give him a parting cheer. And he received a poke of gold as a parting

Packers going up the summit of
Chilcoot Pass during the Gold
Rush, 1898.

PACKERS ASCENDING SUMMIT OF CHILKOOT PASS
COPYRIGHT 1898

Left: A full dress mounted parade on the occasion of the visit of the Duke of Cornwall and York to Calgary – 1901.
Below: A photograph of the North West Mounted Police officers of 'B' Division in Dawson, Yukon Territory, in 1905.

gift from Big Alex McDonald, King of the Klondike.

In his 1894 report, Constantine expressed concern about whalers wintering on Herschel Island off the Yukon's north coast and in the unpoliced Mackenzie to the east. They traded whisky with the natives for 'furs, walrus ivory bone and their young girls.' With things under control in the Yukon, the Force turned its attention to the 'Sodom and Gomorrah of the Ice-Fields.' Sergeant Fitzgerald and Constable Sutherland arrived at Pauline Cove on Herschel Island on 7 August 1903, just in time to greet the whalers.

' A lot of liquor came ashore the first few days,' wrote Sutherland,' but most of it eventually fell into our hands.' In showing the whalers that there was 'a law or two even in the Yukon,' he had to knock one of them 'into two o'clock next summer.' Both he and Fitzgerald often had to pull out their revolvers, but they brought law and order to this wild place, stopped the liquor traffic and collected customs dues. The Inuit and whalers resented their presence, but one of Fitzgerald's main complaints was that he had only four sheets of paper for his report.

The whaling fleets had vanished by 1906 with the discovery of a substitute for whalebone in women's corsets. The Mounties stayed at Herschel Island to take care of the Inuit along the coast and to maintain a Canadian presence in the North.

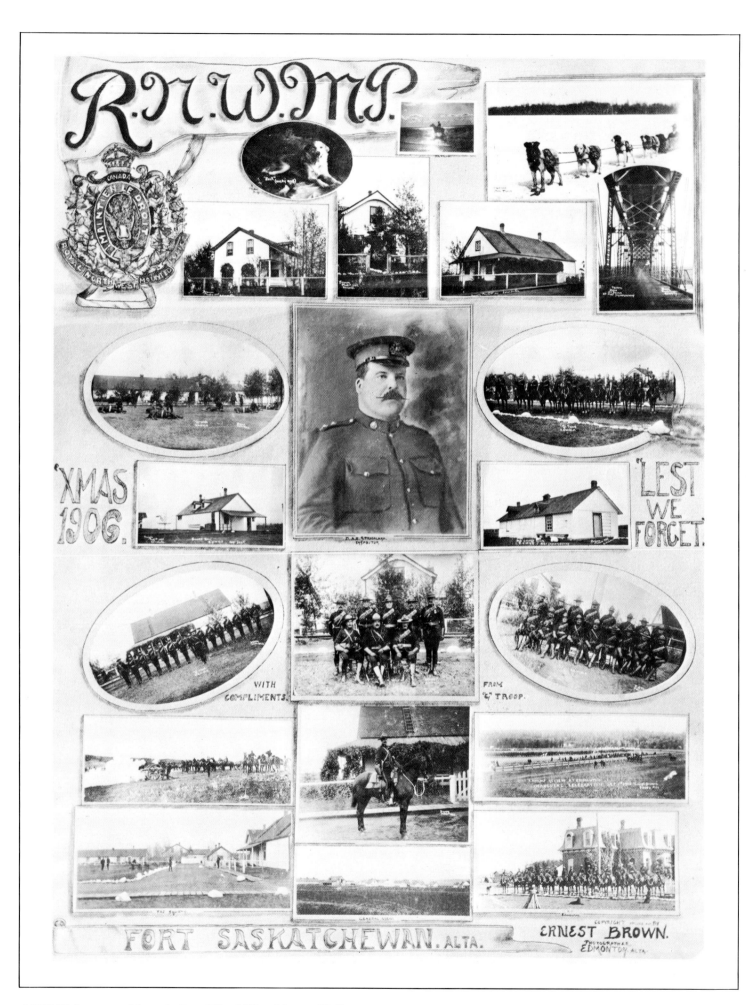

A 1906 Christmas card from the Royal North West Mounted Police.

Police work in the North demanded well-honed minds as well as muscle. Constable Alick Pennycuick, a former British officer, investigated the disappearance of three men who vanished on the trail 50 miles south of Dawson in 1900. In the depths of winter, Pennycuick and an assistant scoured 40 square miles of bush in search of clues. The Mounties had a suspect, George O'Brien, but nothing to link him to the vanished men. Pennycuick found a possible ambush site, and a sled dog pawed the ground nearby. Digging down, the Mountie found a patch of frozen blood. He sent for O'Brien's dog, showed it the blood, and turned it loose. The animal led the Mountie straight to an abandoned riverside camp. Here Pennycuick sifted through the snow, finding charred clothing, cartridge cases, a skull fragment, and a broken tooth embedded in a bullet. When the ice melted in the spring, the Yukon river gave up its dead. In the jawbone of one of the three missing men was a tooth stump that fitted the fragment found by Pennycuick. O'Brien was convicted and hung, and Pennycuick became known as 'the Sherlock Holmes of the Mounted Police.'

Among its responsibilities, the Force carried the mail throughout the Arctic. In December 1904, Corporal Mapley, two constables and a guide left Dawson on a mail patrol, crossed the Mackenzie Mountains and reached Fort McPherson on the Peel River a month later, after a run of 475 miles through empty country. This winter patrol became an accepted part of the Force's life, but just before the outbreak of the First World War, a tragedy on the trail showed just how dangerous life in the North could be, how small the margin for error.

The annual patrol for 1910 left Fort McPherson on 10 December, led by Inspector Francis Fitzgerald, a former shoe salesman from Halifax, Nova Scotia, who had joined the Force in 1888 and had only recently been commissioned. With him went Constables Kinney and Taylor, and Special Constable Sam Carter, an ex-Mountie hired as a guide. They took few provisions with them in order to make better time. Carter claimed to know the trail to Dawson, but the party turned up the wrong valley in the Wind River country, floundered around in temperatures that reached wind chill values of −100°F and then backtracked to Fort McPherson as their supplies ran out.

An Indian who helped them along the way reported this fact to the police in Dawson, who became alarmed and sent out a search party under Constable Dempster in February 1911. In March it picked up the trail of the Lost Patrol, finding empty corned beef cans and a piece of a flour sack. Farther on they came across an abandoned toboggan, harness and dog bones. A flag fluttering from a tree on a river bank led the searchers to the bodies of the two younger men. Kinney had died of starvation, Taylor had shot himself.

Racked by starvation, their skins peeling from frostbite and scurvy, Fitzgerald and Carter had pushed on. The guide died first. Fitzgerald crossed Carter's hands on his chest, placed a handkerchief over his face, and then lay down and died – only 25 miles from Fort McPherson. He

Top: George O'Brien of the infamous O'Brien murder case – 1899.
Above: Fred Clayson – the victim in the O'Brien Murder case.

had written out his last will and testament with a charred stick, ending it 'God Bless All.' Then he signed his name, and added 'R.N.W.M.P.'

The men of the patrol had been selected to attend the Coronation of King George V that summer. The British government had recognized the value of the Force by allowing it in June 1904 to prefix its title with the word 'Royal.'

The highway that now runs from just east of Dawson and north across the Arctic Circle to Fort McPherson carries the name of Constable Dempster. And on a bridge in Halifax's Public Gardens, a plaque commemorates Inspector Fitzgerald: 'Who lost his life while serving his country on the trail in the Yukon Territory.'

Chapter **8**

NEW PROVINCES, NEW PROBLEMS

By the end of the 19th century, the Mounties had made life on the western and northern frontiers secure.

In 1897, a contingent of the NWMP attended Queen Victoria's Diamond Jubilee. Wearing felt hats, red cloth tunics, blue breeches and black boots, and carrying Winchester rifles, they personified the glamour and dash of the high noon of Empire and the dominance of the British over 'lesser breeds without the Law.'

Through vigorous action, Herchmer had created a modern police force. The Force granted leave to officers and men to serve in the Boer War in Strathcona's Horse and the Canadian Mounted Rifles. On 5 July 1900, Sergeant A H L Richardson, a former Mountie, won the Victoria Cross for rescuing a comrade under fire.

When Commissioner Aylesworth Perry took over as head of the Force in 1900 he faced different problems from those of his predecessors. The needs of the settlers on the prairies had to be met, and the Force moved into a new frontier in the Arctic and north of the lands suitable for agriculture. Perry had been a superintendent at 25, and was only 40 when he became commissioner, a post he held for 22 years. He piloted the RNWMP through the difficult constitutional and political shoals as it became Canada's national police force.

Most of the 'Originals' died, retired or went elsewhere during his tenure. Constable Donkin, who had enlisted in 1884, died penniless and broken in health in a workhouse in northern England in 1890. Others stayed in the west as

Above: A telegraph office at Battle Creek, about 1885.
Opposite: Aylesworth Perry, Commissioner of the Mounties from 1 August 1900 to 31 March 1923.

ranchers and government officials. Sam Steele commanded Strathcona's Horse, remained in South Africa to train the constabulary and became a major-general and a knight before his death on 30 January 1919.

In 1905, a party under Superintendent Constantine left Fort Saskatchewan to build a road from the Peace River country to the Yukon – with axes. They cleared timber and built bridges, carving a route over mountains, down valleys and through swamps, completing 375 miles of trail, until the government lost interest and abandoned the project after three years. Constantine's remarkable career has never received the attention lavished on that of Sam Steele; his Yukon diaries were found in the open at Fortymile when the community was being renovated a few years ago. Constantine, much admired by his men as a character, died aged 63 in 1912, in Long Beach, California. The Alaska Highway follows the route the Force pioneered.

Between 1902 and 1913, 500 Mounties purchased their discharge, 500 were dismissed for cause, 350 left when their time expired – and 500 deserted. In 1901, the Force numbered only 761, and the heavy turnover resulted from the poor pay and the strenuous conditions of work.

Constables started at 60 cents a day, and it took them eight years to reach $1 a day – the starting wage for a hired hand on a prairie farm. Pinkerton detectives earned $8 a day for doing the same sort of work as the Mounties. And they did not have to carry out the wide range of duties that the Force had to undertake as the prairies became populated. Their barracks served as post offices, and they carried mail, acted as agents for the Indian Department, collected customs, wrote reports on crops and soils, took weather observations, carried out censuses, transported men who had gone mad to the Brandon Asylum, and enforced a wide range of ordinances, including those covering stallions-at-large and leprosy. The Force's surgeons, often the only doctors available, treated Indians and settlers.

As one Mounted Policeman remarked, 'When people had taken up land, they were too busy to get into trouble.' One settler ordered a police patrol off his land because their horses were eating his valuable grass. One man bought some cattle and left them unbranded and unwatched in a pasture. When they disappeared, he talked of bringing an action against the police. The officer at Fort Macleod wrote caustically that whether the action was for 'allowing him to lose his beasts or for failing to find them I know not.' Members of the Force tried to encourage the settlers to co-operate in the building of fire breaks to protect their isolated farms, but many refused to do so. In October 1905, Constable Conradi saw fire sweeping towards Battleford, and learned that a farm lay in its path. He rode out and helped the farmer to finish ploughing a fire break. The flames leapt this and raced towards a slough where the farmer, his wife and ten children had taken refuge. Conradi dashed through the flames, picked up two children, and led the family to safety. He was badly burned – and his horse had to be destroyed the next morning.

Because of the shortage of recruits, the Force opened an office in London, England, and by 1914, about 80% of its members came from Britain. The recruits included a hypnotist, an individual who'd been the Wild Man of Borneo in a circus, and public school graduates. The Force also recruited young specialists. Vernon Kemp, son of an impecunious preacher, joined the Mounties in 1910 at the age of 15 as a stenographer. He retired 35 years later as Assistant Commissioner. The Force also relied on Indian and Métis scouts, who had the powers of police officers, but no uniforms. In his memoirs, Kemp recalls

the names of these forgotten men – Roland Takes-Wood-in-the-Night, Tom Tail-Feathers-around-his-Neck, and William Never-Ties-his-Shoestrings.

In the years before World War One, the Mounties developed an individualistic and freewheeling style. One Mountie became a fur trader and another sold sewing machines on patrol. On one occasion, three men returning to barracks after a night on the town decided to determine if all was well with the post's mascot – a black bear. It was hibernating at the time, so they dug the animal out of its snow den – and it promptly fell asleep in the road. Touched with compassion, they carried it to the barracks and left it to sleep on the vacant bed of the night guard.

The range of duties carried out by the Force at this time is illustrated by the experiences of William Parker in February 1903. He travelled 500 miles northeast of Prince Albert to arrest an Indian woman for the murder of her stepson. 'It was a hard, cold trip,' he recalls, with temperatures of 40 below zero and snow three feet deep. At Pelican Narrows, the Indians were starving, but on the Churchill River Parker encountered a Métis trapper with a catch of furs worth $10,000. He found the woman, and arrested her. Parker, an inspector and Justice of the Peace, then had her brought before him. The stepson had run away and frozen to death. Those who dressed the body for burial swore that it carried no marks, and the Indian mother was acquitted.

Opposite: A Royal North West Mounted Police patrol about to leave Dawson for Fort McPherson – 26 December 1909.
Below: A Royal North West Mounted Police drill squad at Regina, Saskatchewan in 1908.

A few days later, Parker helped a large group of 'a refined class of settlers.' The Barr colonists had been persuaded by their leader to establish an agricultural settlement in western Canada – but few had any knowledge of farming. The government reserved a stretch of virgin land for them near the present city of Lloydminster, Saskatchewan. Parker gave them information and advice. A party bought a yoke of oxen, alleged to be young and sound. The Mounties examined them, and found them to be 20 years old. The vendor, 'on being interviewed,' replaced them with a younger team.

The Mounties had also to protect buildings and property at Lethbridge, Alberta, during a strike and guard five men with smallpox to ensure they remained in quarantine when the disease hit a small village near Medicine Hat. When a huge rockslide smashed through the town of Frank in the Crow's Nest Pass in the early morning of 29 April 1903, Mounted Police led the rescue operation, turning the local detachment into a hospital. When a coal mine at Hill Crest, Alberta, exploded in June 1914 with the loss of 188 lives, the local Mountie detachment closed the local hotel to head off drunkenness, kept order at the mine mouth, secured the money and property of the dead miners and then washed and wrapped the bodies.

Much of the work of the Force was monotonous. But the possibility of violent death was ever present. A German count who had issued bogus cheques, taken into custody in Saskatoon, committed suicide with prussic acid from a bottle bandaged under his armpit – while in the same bed as the Mountie guarding him. During the summer of 1904, a Mountie stopped to spend the night at a settler's house. He dropped his revolver, which went off and killed him. While patrolling Frank, Alberta, in April 1908, Constable Willmot challenged a prowler who killed him with a shotgun blast. The Mounties traced the killer and brought him to trial – in 1912.

The myth that the motto of the Force is 'We always get our man' grew out of a statement by the Fort Benton *Record* that the Mounties 'fetched their man every time' when they went after whisky traders. When a chinook wind exposed the body of a murdered man, the only clue to his identity was the word 'Kalamazoo' on his suspender buckle. Sergeant Hetherington traced the man – and his killer.

In 1902, the Calgary police arrested Ernest Cashel of Wyoming on charges of forgery. He escaped from custody, and the Mounties went after him. Then a rancher vanished. Through careful detective work, Constable Pennycuick linked Cashel to the rancher's disappearance and the killer died on the gallows at Calgary on 15 December 1903.

Another case had the flavour of 'High Noon' about it. The Idaho Kid arrived in Weyburn in May 1903, and began to terrorize the town, parading down the main street and shooting at verandahs and the hat of a citizen. If any Mounted Policeman tried to stop him, he claimed, 'he'd eat his liver cold.' The terrified townspeople wired the nearest NWMP detachment: 'Come up next train

party running amuck with revolver.' Constable Lett arrived on the next freight train. But the angry citizens refused to help him. By this time the Idaho Kid had retired to a hotel room with his wife. Lett knocked down the door and jumped the man before he could reach for his gun. After a fierce fight in which the Kid's wife participated, Lett clapped handcuffs on the man and led him away.

Just before the outbreak of war, a charge was laid before a Justice of the Peace in Northern Alberta concerning a man's abduction of a 15-year-old girl. Sergeant Charles Harper set off after the couple who had fled into the Rockies. He travelled 700 miles in the middle of winter, found the abductor – and discovered that the girl had gone willingly with him. Harper arrested the man, who received a stern lecture from the judge – and a suspended sentence.

In 1905, the Force handled 4647 criminal cases. Six years later, constables on patrol had to cover 2000 square miles, and in 1912 they secured 11,435 convictions in 13,394 cases.

When Alberta and Saskatchewan became provinces in 1905, two hundred Mounties put on an impressive display of horsemanship at the inauguration ceremonies at Edmonton and Regina. In the Northwest Territories, the Force had been responsible for enforcing territorial ordinances, criminal laws and federal statutes. In the new provinces, provincial and criminal laws became the responsibility of attorneys general. In 1906, Commissioner Perry met with provincial authorities to discuss the future of the Force. Alberta and Saskatchewan agreed to retain the services of the RNWMP for five years. The Mounties would maintain a minimum of 250 men in each province, which would pay the federal government $75,000 a year for their services. The Force remained under Ottawa, but came under the direction of provincial attorneys general where the administration of criminal laws and provincial statutes was concerned.

In 1911, the contracts were renewed – but without any increase in the number of Mounties. The small number of officers and the large areas they had to cover meant that Mounties had wide powers of discretion and some developed highly individualistic ways of handling problems of law and order.

Above: The Royal North West Mounted Police launch *Gladys* at Carcross between Whitehorse and Skagway. She was on duty there from 1906 to 1908.
Right: A patrol under Corporal W J Dempster (left) about to leave Dawson in search of a lost patrol – 28 February 1911.

As one Mountie put it, 'we were as God made us, and oftentimes even worse.' The Force's members did make mistakes. Young Constable Forbes chased a man who had assaulted his own family and neighbours. With the help of an ex-policeman, he saw a couple of riders on the prairies and galloped after them. Arresting one man, he pushed him into a mudhole, threatening to blow his brains out before handcuffing him to a tree. Then he went to help his companion, who was wrestling with the other man on horseback, and kicked the horse out from under his opponent. It turned out that he'd arrested the wrong man. Forbes wrote in his report: 'But he was very peaceful.'

Chapter 9

SETTLERS AND A WORLD AT WAR

Sergeant Bob Handcock patrolled the area north and east of Prince Albert from a post so isolated that it could only be reached by canoe in summer and by dog team in winter. He used common sense in settling disputes and gained a reputation for a direct style of action – and writing. Indian Thomas had 'displayed undue erotic tendencies' towards the wife of an absent Indian. Since Thomas had been 'mixed up in a fishy deal' on Handcock's last winter patrol, the Mountie told him that 'next time it would come to a proper trial and this was his last chance.' On another occasion, he settled a problem quickly when an Indian shot at a neighbour's dog: 'I found the complainant had left his dogs to rustle for themselves, so he was as much to blame. I gave them both a lecture in general.'

Handcock wrote of one patrol, 'I was fortunate in getting a good dog in exchange for the one I purchased at the start of the patrol. I was tired of yelling at him . . . The trail was fierce . . . One can imagine the trouble, and, may I say, the language that necessarily follows.'

The personality of the first four commissioners shaped the style of the Force in its first quarter century. Over the next two decades, the individual acts of Mounties created a legend about their efficiency and responsiveness. As the Western world inched towards war, the Force had to confront threats to law and order posed by organized groups. When dealing with native peoples, they showed an appreciation of how these societies handled threats to

Above: Sergeant Casey Edgerton (left) and Interpreter and Guide Gerard Chisigallok, an Eskimo from Hershel Island, at Fort MacPherson. *Opposite:* Royal North West Mounted Police officers and NCOs in a class for overseas (Siberia) squadrons in Regina in 1917.

79

their existence. But when groups were inspired by foreign religious and political ideologies, the Mounties had to sort out whether they were more of a danger to the state than to themselves.

In March 1907, Constables O'Neill and Cashman travelled for two months north of Lake Winnipeg to investigate reports of killings of Indians at Sandy Lake. They were the first white men the Indians had ever seen. The Mounties found that the Cree tied the mouths of their dogs to prevent them from eating fish bones, practised polygamy, and strangled anyone who fell sick and became delirious in case the evil spirits infecting them scared the game. The Mounties lectured the Indians on the care of their dogs, and arrested two medicine men who strangled the sick people. One committed suicide and the other died in hospital.

On the prairies, many of the newcomers from Galicia, Sweden, Germany, Finland, Russia and other places built their own settlements, instead of adopting the individualistic pattern of settlement favoured by settlers from Britain, the United States and eastern Canada. When Sam Steele served on the prairies he became upset by Mormons who practised polygamy, and suggested that the group be put under surveillance. Fred White rejected the idea, and Steele did note that these people had the most prosperous and successful farms in the area.

Of the groups that settled in the West, only the Doukhobors gave the Mounted Police any trouble. They had emigrated from Russia in the 1890s after coming into conflict with the government. Their laws came from God, not from man, they claimed, and they refused to obey any rules and regulations they disliked. With the help of the Canadian government, groups of Doukhobors settled in Saskatchewan in 1905. At first they stayed on their farms and remained quiet. But then they took to the countryside in bursts of religious ecstasy, wandering around naked and alarming other settlers, who called in the Mounties.

Above: The Royal North West Mounted Police cavalry draft, preparing for service in Siberia-Regina, 1918.
Opposite: The camp of the RNWMP cavalry draft at Regina.
Below: 'B' Squadron of the Royal North West Mounted Police Siberian Expeditionary Force on parade at Regina, shortly before they departed for Siberia – 1918.

'Full band of fanatics perfectly nude marching on Hledoberno singing, wheeling dead woman in truck. Cannot persuade them to make a coffin,' read one telegram to Mountie headquarters. The police patiently rounded up the marchers, found their clothes and either persuaded them to dress – or dressed them. On one chilly day, naked men and women tramped across the prairie, searching for Christ. When the police intervened, they agreed to go to the nearest village, but insisted that a Mountie lead them on his horse.

The Mounties acquired a great deal of skill in handling insane individuals on what were known as 'lunatic patrol.' but the religious mania of the Doukhobors sorely tried their patience. In 1908, 20 Doukhobors leapt naked from a colonist car in Yorkton, Saskatchewan. The police rounded them up and put them into an agricultural hall while the provincial government made up its mind about what to do with them. When the group was moved to tents in a fenced enclosure, the police tried to remove 12 of them to an insane asylum. Some Doukhobors resisted, then went on a hunger strike. The police had to force feed them, but finally persuaded the group to eat.

Later writers accused the Mounties of 'police brutality' on such occasions. The Reverend R G Macbeth wrote a history of the Force in 1921, entitled *Policing the Plains*, which captures the essence of life in the West in those days. He recalls coming across a little frontier encampment – 'characteristic outfit with lax ideas in regard to laws which touched upon personal desires as to gambling, strong drink, Sunday trading and the rest.' The residents had a habit of fleecing unwary travellers and lonely settlers. Then, one day, into the shack town rode 'a young athlete in a uniform of silver and gold.' He issued a few warnings, tacked up a notice or two, then saddled his rested steed and cantered over the plain, after 'a sudden air of orderliness settled on the locality.'

The constable, a resident informed Macbeth, was 'the embodiment of the Empire which plays no favourites but which at the same time will stand no nonsense from anyone.'

When eastern Europeans began to settle in the west, Reverend Macbeth noted that since they were 'unacquainted with our institutions and disposed to bring with them a sort of hatred of authority born of experience under old-world despotisms' they needed 'the educative and restraining influence of . . . the riders in scarlet and gold.' Otherwise their newly-found liberty 'would soon degenerate into licence.'

Sergeant Ben Belcher provided an example of this educative and restraining influence as war broke out. With a constable, he entered a hotel where a drunken orator was haranguing a crowd of Germans. The man greeted them with: '*Hoch der Kaiser!* Red-coated swine.' Belcher ploughed his way through the crowd, slugged the orator, and dragged him to the door. Here he turned and said: 'And the rest of you'll get the same treatment if you start hocking the bloody Kaiser round here.'

About 200,000 Germans and Austrians had settled on the prairies, and the people there began seeing spies everywhere and calling in the Mounties. The Force registered all 'enemy aliens' in Alberta and Saskatchewan, confiscated their weapons, but arrested only 396 of them and put another 326 on parole.

In 1915, the RNWMP acquired its first car, a McLaughlin, to transport prisoners in Regina. More cars and motorcycles helped them to patrol the international boundary during the following year when the Canadian government learned of plans by pro-German elements in the United States to cross the border, stir up discontent among German and Austrian settlers and sabotage the Canadian Pacific Railway. The Force's numbers quickly rose from 500 to 1200 officers and men, but with the entry

A group of senior NCOs at Vladivostock – 1918.

of America into the war in 1917, the threat from the United States disappeared.

During the war years, the Mounties also had to fight the demon drink. In 1915, the government of Saskatchewan closed the bars, and in the same year the province voted in prohibition. The Mounted Police chased bootleggers and enforced the liquor ordinances, a task they disliked on its own merits, and because it threatened morale and discipline. At the beginning of the war, the government refused to release any of the police for duty with the armed forces. Only 50 British recruits were allowed to rejoin their regiments on mobilization.

Alberta and Saskatchewan had formed small police forces to administer the liquor regulations, and these slowly grew in size, especially after the Mounties concentrated their efforts on guarding the international boundary. On 1 January 1917, the Mounties were relieved of their provincial policing duties in Saskatchewan and Manitoba, and in the following year they transferred responsibility for these duties to provincial police in Alberta.

About 1000 Mounties whose time had elapsed or who purchased their discharges had joined the forces. With the decline in their duties and the heavy losses on the Western front, the Mounted Police were called upon to provide reinforcements for the Canadian Cavalry Brigade and to provide a distinct Police unit for the Cavalry Corps. About 700 Mounties signed up for overseas service early in 1918 – although only 500 had been requested. In England, the contingent lost its identity as members were posted to various units, but a Mounted Police Squadron formed part of the Canadian Light Horse in France, and in October an independent unit called the Royal North-West Mounted Police Squadron came into being. The Mounties played a valuable role as dispatch riders and in guarding prisoners.

Various regulation uniforms of the Force – 1919.

This page: Three members of the Royal North West Mounted Police detachment at Drumheller, Alberta in 1919.
Opposite: A photograph of the RCMP 'H' Division at Regina prior to relocating in Vancouver – 1920.

Late in 1917, the British Government asked Canada to send troops to Siberia to fight the Bolsheviks. Commissioner Perry recruited 190 officers and men who volunteered, and on 1 October 1918, their squadron officially became part of the Canadian Expeditionary Force (Siberia); 21 members arrived in Vladivostock with the advance party in the same month.

Like most of the rest of the expeditionary force, the Mounties saw no action in Russia. When the Canadian troops embarked for Vancouver in April 1919, six Mounties stayed behind to deliver their horses to the White Russians at Ekaterinburg. Under Farrier Sergeant Margetts, they crossed Russia in 38 days. The decision to leave the horses proved unpopular, as some of the Mounties had ridden them on detachment on the prairies.

By the time of the November armistice, the Force in Canada had shrunk to 303 men, half of whom served in the Yukon and Northwest Territories. And the Bolshevik Revolution had an impact on them. The Force had always used undercover people to identify troublemakers before they made trouble, and to obtain the sort of information not readily available through overt means. In 1917, together with military intelligence, the Mounties started surveillance of radical organizations because of their opposition to conscription and the fear that the Russian revolution would inspire a similar uprising in western Canada. RNWMP agents infiltrated the mineworkers' union in Drumheller and heard Italians declare that they would shut down the pits. They also moved into British Columbia and kept an eye on radicals there. By early 1919, the police and the military become convinced that a revolution was about to break out in the West, and military intelligence officers stressed the need to take a hard line with the workers.

Winnipeg was the key city.

Here the Trades and Labour Council called a general strike in May 1919. The Army and the RNWMP prepared to halt an insurrection as the city ceased to function, and strikes spread across the country. The Mounties arrested some of the ringleaders of the strike in mid-June. On 21 June 1919, about 50 Mounties moved out of barracks to halt an illegal parade in the centre of Winnipeg. Two troops rode up Main Street, scattering the crowd. As they returned down Portage, shots were fired at them, and bricks, concrete chunks and bottles flew through the air. Three Mounties were pulled or knocked from their horses, and the others regrouped, drew their revolvers, and fired a volley over the heads of the crowd, which failed to disperse. Then they shot low, killing one man, fatally wounding another and injuring several more. In all 30 people were injured during the Winnipeg riot – including 16 Mounted Policemen. As S W Horrall, the Force's historian, put it in his centennial history: 'It was an ugly and tragic event which none regretted more than those members of the Force who took part in it.'

This incident laid the foundations of the mistrust that labour groups and radical organizations have of the Force. On 7 June 1922, R H Butts, a Member of Parliament for Cape Breton, Nova Scotia, said in the House of Commons that 'If the government sends the Mounted Police down there [to Cape Breton] these men will not only be unappreciated but they will be regarded as intruders.'

The government learned the lesson of Winnipeg, but still believed that men on horseback were the best means of keeping radicals in check. When tensions rose among miners and steelworkers in Cape Breton in the 1920s, the central government sent other mounted men to preserve law and order – the Royal Canadian Dragoons and the Royal Canadian Horse Artillery.

At the beginning of the 1920s, it looked as if the Mounties might simply become a group to enforce internal security. The introduction of prohibition in the United States and an upsurge in crime in Canada rescued them from this fate.

Meanwhile they added to their laurels by their work in the Arctic where they brought law and order – and the presence of the Dominion government – to a vast and sparsely populated region.

Chapter 10
ARCTIC MEN

Above: Supply sleds of 'N' Division at Lesser Slave Lake in 1909.
Opposite: The Headquarters of the GMP Hershel Island Detachment – 1924-25.

Beyond the limits of settlement in Canada lies a land unlike any other on earth. The boreal forest, which covers most of the Yukon, gives way to the tundra, a place of rock and ice and snow, inhabited at the end of the 19th century by bands of wandering Inuit. These people lived on the edge of survival in a harsh land that had little margin for error. Explorers penetrated into the Arctic by sea and came equipped with all the accoutrements of their civilizations. But this did not prevent the loss of the entire Franklin Expedition in 1848. Those who succeeded in finding the remains of its members used the techniques of travel developed by the Inuit. They did not seek to impose their ways upon this huge and empty land.

Many of the seekers after the Franklin Expedition wrote books telling of their trials and tribulations in the Arctic. When the Mounties approached the Arctic, they did so the hard way – overland. Some of their patrols rank with those of the explorers in distances travelled, the amount of new land visited and the hardships endured. Explorers turned to them for help on a number of occasions. When Raold Amundsen, the first man to sail a ship through the Northwest Passage, needed dogs, he sent an Inuk to the police post at Fullerton in 1905 for them. The Mounties obliged by supplying ten animals. Thirteen years late, Vilhjalmur Stefansson, leader of the Canadian Arctic Expedition and proponent of the concept of 'The Friendly Arctic,' staggered into the RNWMP post at Herschel Island, sick with typhoid. The Mounties there

Above: Some members of the crew aboard the RCMP Police Boat *Chakawana*, about 1920.
Right: Indians in full dress with members of the Calgary Detachment of the Royal Canadian Mounted Police during the Calgary Stampede of 1924.

nursed him back to health, but Constable Lamont caught the disease and died on 16 February 1918.

Herschel Island, the far western anchor of the Force's northern presence, had relatively easy access by sea and could also be reached by travelling down the Mackenzie Valley. To the east lay the Barren Grounds of the mainland north of the prairie provinces, and the scatter of Arctic Islands where land and sea merged under a cover of white for most of the year. At the end of the 19th century, a patrol crossed Lake Winnipeg and reached York Factory on Hudson Bay, and a line of posts in northern Alberta checked freight and prevented liquor from moving into the Mackenzie District.

The Force moved into the central Arctic in September 1903, when Superintendent John Moodie arrived with five men at Fullerton on the northwest coast of Hudson Bay. Only whalers, a few traders and scattered bands of Inuit occupied the central Arctic at that time. The Mounties built a post, and one man went mad during the winter, filling the cramped quarters with his screams. Moodie returned to Ottawa in the following year, but was sent back north with more men to set up 'M' Division covering the whole Hudson Bay region. The next winter passed 'quickly and pleasantly,' he reported. Constable Seller travelled 500 miles north of the post in February 1906 to inspect whaling operations in Repulse Bay and Lyon's

Inlet. The whalers, mainly Scots, proved to be a sober lot and they left the Arctic when the market for whalebone collapsed.

To the west, the Force set up 'N' Division in 1905, with headquarters at Athabaska Landing on Lesser Slave Lake; it covered northern Alberta and the Mackenzie District. Patrols from here and Fullerton covered large areas, and the Mounties adopted the Inuit way of travelling in winter.

But Inspector Pelletier and three Mounties chose the summer of 1908 to link up the two northern detachments. They left Athabaska Landing in June and headed north by scow to Great Slave Lake. Paddling a canoe across Great

Slave Lake, they then staggered over 63 miles of portage, under a blazing sun and bitten by hordes of mosquitoes, and launched their boat in Artillery Lake. Here they saw a wondrous sight – thousands of caribou swarmed around the body of water. Late in July they met a band of Indians, the last humans they would see until they neared Hudson Bay. The route to there lay down unknown rivers. Paddling down the Hanbury, Pelletier reported, 'The water is good and fast, making it very exciting going down. There are many sharp bends and very short stretches are seen at a time, thereby adding more zest to the adventure.' On the Barren Grounds they encountered musk-oxen, and, finally, a few Inuit, whom Pelletier

The Ross Mark II Military Rifle
is Without Equal for Speed.

The Ross Mark II – the issue rifle from 1909 to 1912, Calibre 3.03. A British piece with a five round capacity.

described as 'a jolly lot.' The party shot the rapids on the Lower Thelon and Schultz Rivers – 'one of the most exciting experiences of the trip' – and reached the shores of Hudson Bay on 31 August.

But their adventures had not ended.

The Fullerton detachment sent a whaleboat down to meet the patrol. At Marble Island, near the mouth of Chesterfield Inlet, the Mounties hunted walrus. A disgruntled animal holed a skiff carrying two of the hunters, and Constable Donaldson drowned in the icy waters of the bay. When the party from Fullerton linked up with Pelletier's group, the inspector set off south in the whale boat. A storm wrecked it, and he turned back to Fullerton. In November Pelletier set off overland with five men, 17 dogs and two sleds. Hit by storms, the party ran out of food and coal oil before reaching Churchill on 11 January 1909. The inspector then headed for Gimli, Manitoba, by dog team, completing a patrol of 3347 miles.

In his report, Pelletier suggested that there was no need for permanent yearly patrols, or for a post farther north than Churchill, which had become 'M' Division headquarters in 1906. The area did not need game laws – but a proper vessel would be useful in collecting customs dues on Hudson Bay. And Pelletier added in his report, 'At no time on the journey were we in a precarious position.'

As Europe moved towards war, news filtered out of the Arctic about the killing of two explorers and two priests by the Inuit. Radford and Street had last been seen alive in mid-summer, 1912, and Fathers Rouvier and Leroux had travelled north in the fall of 1913 to live among the Copper Eskimos. An Inuk reported the deaths of the first two outsiders, and a Dog Rib Indian told of an Inuk seen wearing a blood-stained cassock with a hole over the heart. The murders had taken place in the Bathurst Inlet-Coronation Gulf area in the remote central Arctic.

And so the Mounties set out to investigate the killings.

Inspector Beyts and three other Mounties established a detachment at Chesterfield Inlet in July 1914 and tried to reach Bathurst Inlet from the east. On a patrol through 'the hardest country to travel in that I have experienced in the Force,' as Beyts put it, the inspector and his men suffered great hardships. The oil-stove failed; huskies died of sheer exhaustion, ate their harnesses and tore each other to pieces; the tent caught fire; natives failed to put up caches of dog food for return trips. One patrol accidentally split, and for two nights Beyts had no bed and nothing to eat except biscuits. In this empty land, the patrol shot seven caribou, planted a cache and returned to base after travelling 585 miles in 52 days. Beyts concluded that it was impossible to reach Bathurst Inlet under such conditions.

Inspector 'Denny' La Nauze, placed in charge of the search for the missing priests, learned of the location of their cabin from D'Arcy Arden, an English trader, who had found everything inside 'in terrible shape.' La Nauze headed north from Great Bear Lake in April 1916, reached the site of the cabin on Dease River, and built winter quarters nearby. Meanwhile, Corporal Bruce from Herschel Island worked his way eastward along the coast beyond the Mackenzie Delta and established a base at Bernard Harbour. He met Inuit who put up his tent, fed his dogs, brought him fresh caribou meat and took away his boots to be dried and mended. Then they dressed him in native costume, took him to the large skin tent that served as a dance hall and asked him to bang the big drum. The Mountie finally made contact with the Inuit group whose members had killed the two priests, and then linked up with La Nauze at Coronation Gulf. Here they learned of the fate of the missing priests. Rouvier and Leroux had been 'good white men,' said the Inuit and 'very good to us.' But they coveted their meagre possessions, and the priests must have sensed their greed. One day they fled, and two Inuit, Sinnisiak and Uluksak, went in pursuit. At Bloody Falls on the Coppermine River, the Inuit stabbed one priest and shot the other. Bruce arrested Sinnisiak on south Victoria Island on 15 May 1916, and La Nauze captured Uluksak northeast of the Coppermine eight days later. When asked if he knew why the police had arrested him, Uluksak replied, 'Oh, yes, I know well. Are you going to kill me?'

The Inuit, tried and found guilty, were condemned to death, but their sentences were commuted to life imprisonment. After a few years at Fort Resolution, the two men were pardoned. They helped the Mounties to establish a post at Tree River, 65 miles east of the Coppermine, in 1919. Sinnisiak worked so well that he became a 'special.' Uluksak, a 'troublesome person,' boasted that he wouldn't mind killing a white man. After all, he'd only be 'taken outside and given a good time and then sent back.' He was killed by another Inuk in 1924.

While searching for the killers of the priests, La Nauze came across evidence of the fate of Radford and Street. Radford, the Inuit told him, 'was always angry when travelling' and had taken a whip to an Inuk who refused to march. Street took the whip away, but helped his companion to drag the Inuk towards open water to frighten him. The other Inuit rushed the explorers and knifed them to death.

In March 1917, Inspector French set out to find the killers. He started from Baker Lake in the Barren Grounds, passing through sudden blizzards that blotted out the landscape and sudden sunny spells that melted the party's igloo. Finally he reached the ice of the Northwest Passage, and picked up the trail of an Inuit group – five years after the deaths of Radford and Street. French described the natives as 'very friendly,' identified the three killers, and decided not to arrest them because the two whites had provoked them. Instead he explained the white man's laws to the band.

In the late fall, the party headed south, with few supplies and in the hope of living off the land. At times it looked as if this might be French's last patrol. Dogs raided the stores during a blizzard and ate all the caribou meat. Fortunately the party came across a small herd of caribou which had died of exhaustion as it tried to struggle out of heavy snow. By 4 December French was recording 'clothing and bedding wet and frozen and all feeling the cold

Interpreter-Guide
Nakoopeanpia with Corporals
Stallworthy and Dersch at the
police camp on Tennyson
Cape, Ellesmere Island, 1933.

very much.' Abandoning sleds and shooting dogs to feed to the others, the party reached the tree line three weeks later. Here they found the tracks of musk-oxen, and killed 20 of these great, shaggy beasts. French noted, 'General feeling in camp much better, as regards our dog food and self.' As they struggled towards Baker Lake, the patrol 'reduced to soup only, all meats finished,' cached everything and made a dash for the settlement. They killed ten caribou before finally reaching Baker Lake on 26 January 1918. French had been on patrol for ten months, six of them on the trail, and covered 5153 miles – the longest patrol ever made by the Force.

In the 1920s, police posts joined the Hudson's Bay Company buildings and the lonely homes of Catholic and Anglican priests throughout the central and western Arctic. The Force also went to northern Baffin Island, and posts arose in the uninhabited High Arctic because of Canada's fear that Denmark would claim it. An expedition led by Otto Sverdrup, a Dane, had explored this area in 1898-1902, and the Greenlander Knud Rasmussen, who visited Ellesmere Island in 1919, described it as 'No Man's Land.' The Canadian Government also learned that Greenlanders had been killing musk-oxen in the eastern Arctic, and felt the need to show the flag.

In 1921, Staff Sergeant Joy established a post at Pond Inlet, and set off to investigate the death of a Newfoundland trader. He had the powers of a Justice of the Peace, coroner, customs officer and postmaster. He found the trader's body, disinterred it, and conducted an autopsy. The man had threatened to shoot some Inuit and their dogs, so they selected his executioner. Joy identified the murderer and two accomplices, issued warrants for their arrest, arrested the men, held a preliminary enquiry and committed them to trial. Two of the Inuit were found guilty, and one acquitted.

The Mounties had been favourably impressed with the Inuit on first acquaintance. Inspector Jarvis described the 'Esquimaux' as 'near as God's Chosen people as any I have ever seen' and he almost wished he'd been born one.

As the Force penetrated deeper into the Arctic, its members encountered the dark side of Inuit life. Some killings, such as that on the Belcher Islands in 1920, arose from the need of a community to protect itself from dangerous people. But others resulted from personal quarrels, greed and other motives. Alikomiak killed another Inuk at Tree River in a shoot-out started by a man intent on stealing the wives of others. Corporal Doak arrested him, and since the detachment at Tree River lacked cells, the Inuk remained under open arrest. He had frozen his feet, which Doak carefully tended. 'The general docility of the Eskimo tends to induce white men to trust them,' Doak reported. On 1 April 1922, Alikomiak crept into the Corporal's room and shot him with a rifle. Then he killed a Hudson's Bay Company factor. For these murders he died on the gallows on Herschel Island on 1 February 1924, one of the first two Inuit to be executed.

In the same year, the wife of Staff Sergeant Clay died under tragic circumstances at Chesterfield Inlet. To alleviate the loneliness of northern postings, the Force permitted wives to accompany their husbands to isolated posts. After Margaret Clay's husband went on patrol, she fell among the settlement dogs, to which anything on the ground is food. They stripped the flesh from one of her legs. A priest from the mission amputated the leg, and it looked as if she might recover. Then she sank into a coma and died.

Constable Stallworthy had rescued Mrs Clay from the dogs and prepared the instruments and dressings for the amputation. In the 1930s, this Mountie joined the ranks of the great Arctic explorers. To curb the activities of Greenland poachers, the Force opened posts opposite Greenland on Ellesmere Island at Craig Harbour (1922) and Bache Peninsula (1926), and on Devon Island at Dundas Harbour in 1924. From these posts, patrols travelled extensively throughout the High Arctic Islands, and established Canadian sovereignty here. The death of Sverdrup in 1930 ended any lingering doubts about Canada's ownership of the High Arctic.

The Greenlanders arrested for poaching were loath to leave after they'd served their sentences. For them, the time at the police posts had been a pleasure – not a punishment – with good food, shelter and Mounties to look after their dogs.

Explorers continued to travel in the High Arctic Islands.

In 1931, Dr Krueger, a German, and his two companions were reported missing to Corporal Stallworthy at Bache Peninsula. He formed a patrol and set out in search of them, killing a polar bear, fighting through rough ice for six days, and sitting out blizzards. At one place the patrol had to carry their sleds across bare boulders because of the lack of snow. On his way back to the post, Stallworthy fell down a crevasse. 'Fortunately for me it was a small one, about two feet wide at the top. I was jammed at about thirty feet,' he reported.

Krueger was still missing in 1932, and Stallworthy set out with Constables Hamilton and Dersch and nine Inuit to search an area the size of Italy, covering 90,000 square miles. They searched the land and ice west towards Axel Heiberg Island, probing into the fiords along the coasts of Ellesmere Island, crashing through the ice at places, detouring around open water, hauling the sleds up glaciers that provided access to the interior of islands. On 8 April Stallworthy reached the northern tip of Axel Heiberg, and in a cairn built by Robert Peary found a message from Krueger. His party had headed towards Meighen Island to the southwest. Stallworthy continued the search, mapping new land, staving off starvation, and reaching Bache Peninsula after covering 1400 miles in 65 days. He reported that his experiences involved 'no serious hardship' and concluded that Krueger and his party had perished on or near Meighen Island during the winter of 1930-31.

Stallworthy's patrol owed much of its success to the help of the Inuit, and the skills in living off the land that the Mounties had learned from these people. And the leader of one of the most remarkable ventures ever under-

The *St Roch* moored on the west side of Hershel Island, 1935.

Opposite: The crew of the *St Roch*, 1928. Left to right: front row – Engineer Pat Kelly, Insp Vernon Kemp, Cst Jack Foster; second row – Cst M J Olsen, Cst H A Larsen, Sgt F Anderton, Cst W Parry; back row – Cst R W Kells, Cst T G Parslow, Cst F Seeley.
Right: A former Constable, Inspector H A Larsen aboard the *St Roch.*

taken by the Force also discovered how to survive in this harsh and beautiful land from the people whose home it was.

Henry Asbjorn Larsen was the last of the true Arctic men of the Force – and one of the greatest. Born in Norway in 1899, he grew up around boats and caught 'Arctic Fever' at 23 when he went to Herschel Island to navigate a schooner bought by Christian Klengenberg, a trader. He soon became popular with the Inuit, accepting them with courtesy and never expressing disapproval of their ways. They taught him to handle dog teams and hunt seal. He also made friends with members of the Force and learned that the RCMP planned to acquire a boat as a floating detachment and supply ship. He joined the Mounties in 1928, after becoming a Canadian citizen, and was posted as an ordinary seaman to the *St Roch*.

This vessel would become famous as the first ship to traverse the Northwest Passage in both directions, and to circumnavigate North America. An ungainly looking vessel, only 40 feet long, the *St Roch* was crowded, uncomfortable and underpowered, capable of a maximum speed of only eight knots. She had a rounded hull to ride the ice pressure and rolled violently in open water. Larsen became her captain, and sailed her around the Arctic, singing hymns while standing watch. When the ship froze into winter quarters, he went on patrol. Larsen always had in his mind the idea of taking the *St Roch* through the Northwest Passage. In the spring of 1940, he received orders to do so to reassert Canadian sovereignty. Following the southern route, the vessel wintered over twice and reached Halifax in October 1942. During the previous winter, Constable Chartrand died of heart failure. Larsen and another Mountie travelled 800 miles by dog sled to the nearest Catholic mission to ask the priest to bury 'Frenchy' in his Faith. Larsen was that sort of man.

He received orders in 1944 to take his ship from the Atlantic to the Pacific. Rounding up a scratch crew, he sailed through fog and freezing rain along the coast of Labrador, dodging ice floes and bergs. He found open water as he turned the *St Roch* into the Northwest Passage, and decided to take the northern route through the unexplored waters of Melville Sound and Prince of Wales Strait. The ship weathered a September gale at Tuktoyaktuk on the Mackenzie Delta's eastern edge, and Larsen made a dash for Herschel Island. A month later, the *St Roch* docked in Vancouver after a voyage of over 7000 miles in 86 days.

A modest and self-effacing man, Larsen felt himself on hallowed ground in the Arctic. On entering Erebus Bay, he fancied he 'could see the tall majestic ships of Franklin who wintered there 99 years ago.' Larsen retired in 1961, and died three years later; a stretch of water close to where Franklin's men died is named after him. His ship can be seen in the Vancouver Maritime Museum.

The voyages of the *St Roch* received a great deal of publicity and boosted the spirits of war-weary Canadians. The exploits of Stallworthy, Beyts, La Nauze, French, Bruce and Joy have been almost forgotten. But the northern tip of Axel Heiberg, one of the loneliest places in a lonely land, carries the name Cape Stallworthy, in tribute to one of a remarkable band of Arctic travellers and explorers.

Chapter 11

THE DOLDRUM YEARS

On 1 February 1920, the Force changed its name to the Royal Canadian Mounted Police – and almost disappeared as a separate entity. After the war, the government authorized an increase in its strength to 2500, and raised the pay of a constable to $1.75 a day. Old posts, including Fort Macleod and Battleford, closed, while 70 new detachments opened from Fort William, Ontario, to Port Alberni on Vancouver Island. Headquarters moved from Regina to Ottawa, to a cramped office above a ladies' dress shop in a rundown building.

The Liberal Opposition in Parliament had criticized the Conservatives for using the RNWMP during the Winnipeg riots of 1919. When they took office under Mackenzie King in December 1921, they trimmed the Force's number back to 1200 and made plans to combine it with the regular defence forces under the Minister of Militia. The RCMP was relieved of its role of supporting local authorities during strikes, but came under attack from the recently formed Progressive Party and Labour spokesman J S Woodsworth who represented Winnipeg Centre. He moved a motion in the House of Commons that the Force be banished to Canada's outposts in 1922 and another one to disband it in the following year. Other MPs spoke in defence of the Force, and the motions were lost.

Commissioner Perry had noted in 1920, 'The Force is distributed in the way best suited to perform its many duties. It is found along the international boundary . . .

Above: A photo of Cortlandt Starnes taken while he was adjutant of the 65th Regiment of Militia form Québec during the North West Rebellion and prior to his appointment to the RCMP. He later became commissioner, serving from 1923 to 1931.
Opposite: RCMP members stop for tea while on patrol in Canada's Eastern Arctic.

Above: A rum runner boat, the *Cana II*. It was burned at a wharf at Riviere du Loup, Québec in 1931 while refueling.
Right: Another rum runner boat, the *Racine C.*

on or in the vicinity of Indian Reserves . . . It occupies many lonely posts in the North-West Territories and Yukon Territory . . . It is found in centres of population, and at points where industrial activities are vital to the welfare of the nation.' The Force had absorbed the Dominion Police and its duties covered the enforcement of federal laws, the protection of Dominion buildings and navy yards, the intelligence service, maintaining law and order in the Territories and Dominion parks, running a fingerprint bureau and looking after the records of paroled prisoners.

Clifford Harvison joined the Mounties in 1919. His training in Regina resembled that of a member of a cavalry squadron, he recalls in his autobiography *The Horsemen*. But his first assignments show the range of the Force's activities in the 1920s, the doldrum years. He went to Québec and Halifax to look after 'undesirable immigrants,' although he never learned why they were classified this way. With his fellow officers he found sponsors and employment for some of the newcomers.

Harvison next went undercover in Montréal. The Force established an office in that wide-open, graft-ridden city to stop the drug trade. Harvison expected to be making routine enquiries about applicants applying for naturalization; his first evening in Montréal found him on 'The Main,' looking for drug dealers. The Mounties had an ancient Buick for transportation, but no cells, fingerprinting facilities or photographic equipment. They had to rely on the provincial and municipal police for help, and this 'caused many difficulties and frustrations.' Despite Ottawa's parsimony, morale and devotion to duty remained high. The Mounties raided brothels and opium dens, investigated a silk smuggling racket and broke up a gang of counterfeiters.

Much of their work dealt with that perennial problem – booze. While Prohibition lasted in the United States, distilleries in Canada produced 'quantities of liquor sufficient to meet local requirements for hundreds of years – even should the inhabitants take to bathing in the stuff.' The Mounties had to stop its illegal production and transportation across the border. The federal government had no moral qualms about this trade – it simply wanted its share of the profits through taxes.

Harvison infiltrated a gang of bootleggers, paving the way for his colleagues to make a bust. Commissioner Starnes, a French Canadian who replaced Perry in 1923, visited the Montréal detachment and complimented Harvison on his work. He noted that he played a lot of poker with the bootleggers, and recognized this as a legitimate activity. But, Starnes added, Harvison was 'a hell of a poker player. I look at your expense accounts and always you lose. Our recruit training must be slipping.'

Perry had been tall, stately and dignified, in contrast to the short, rotund, temperamental Starnes. 'Jimmy' Starnes once expressed his frustration when someone sent for a Mountie after a bird's nest had been robbed: 'My God! Do I transfer a constable every time a duck quacks?'

Mounties crossed Canada on harvest trains to keep order – and to prevent workers being exploited. On one trip, Harvison suggested that a store owner in northern Ontario lower his prices when the harvest train arrived. The merchant ignored the advice, and it looked as if the workers would riot. The engineer of the train blew his whistle, and started to move. The harvest hands jumped back aboard, and the store owner, seeing his customers vanishing down the track, dropped his prices.

Harvison resigned in 1923, although he later rejoined the Force and became Commissioner in 1960. He wanted

government buildings in Ottawa. Most were married, whereas the majority of Mounties were single. The Dominion Police worked eight-hour shifts, the Mounties all the hours of the day and the night while on a case. Worse still, the Dominion Police did not know how to ride horses, some were over 70, and a number owed their positions to political pull and did not hesitate to complain to their MPs when disciplined by Mountie officers. Kemp recalls seeing two members of 'A' Division, complete with uniform, helmet, brass spike and chain, taking part in a carnival sideshow in Ottawa. They flanked a muscleman who challenged all comers to wrestle with him. When no one took up the offer, one of the 'Mounties' doffed his helmet and tunic, flexed his muscles and offered five dollars to anyone who would fight him for five minutes.

Kemp notes that 'it actually required twenty-five years of patient effort before the two [police forces]were finally welded into one.'

From Ottawa, Kemp moved to Herschel Island in 1927 as officer commanding the western Arctic subdivision. His titles included Postmaster, Agent of the Mining Recorder, Coroner, Registrar of Vital Statistics, Radio Licence Inspector, Deputy of the Public Administrator, Commissioner for the hearing of naturalization applications, and Collector of Customs, and his area stretched from the Alaska boundary to the Boothia Peninsula and included the Mackenzie Delta.

Kemp went on patrol, by sled and on the *St Roch*. With his wife, he bathed the bodies of sick Inuit when a flu epidemic swept through the area. A Mountie at one detachment cared for a blind and crippled Inuk who had been abandoned by his family on the sea ice, dumped off the sled and left to die. But life in the North had its lighter side. The Force carried out the census in the North, and other government departments looked upon them as handy people to count and collect other things. Kemp received requests to enumerate snowshoe rabbits and to collect specimens of 'biting louse.' A department asked for wood specimens and cross sections of trees, so Stallworthy obligingly sent them a chunk of driftwood from the High Arctic. Another agency asked them to plant bean seeds in the tundra to see if they would grow. As Kemp noted, 'The request was filed; so were the beans.' Members of the Force also helped trappers and traders with their Income Tax returns.

Kemp's tour of duty ended and he went back to 'A' Division in Ottawa, and to 'the atmosphere of fire extinguishers and water mains in government departments' which had little appeal after his time in the Arctic.

As the Force struggled through the 1920s with meagre resources, Hollywood began to create myths and legends about them. One film reviewer in 1919 wrote that 'all Canadian heroes belong to the Mounted,' and three years later 23 Mountie movies were released.

While Hollywood showed the Mounties as tough and dedicated individuals, quick with their fists and their guns, the Force modernized and improved its scientific capacities for combatting crime.

to marry, but his pay was only $2 a day; married men received $1.85 extra. Starnes felt that marriage limited the mobility of members, and issued an edict that no man could marry until he'd served seven years: In 1927, the waiting period became 12 years.

And so the Mounties continued to operate as loners.

In 1921, a sad-faced Austrian painter named Jack Esselwein joined the Communist Party of Canada in Regina. Although he never held office, he became a valuable worker for the cause, helping to organize a front called the Workers' Party, and then moving on to Toronto. The Communist Party's manifestoes called for 'the violent overthrow of bourgeois power,' and as economic conditions deteriorated the government acted. In 1931, it began raiding Communist Party officer and arresting key members. When the party members came to trial, the key witness against them was Jack Esselwein who was Sergeant John Leopold of the RCMP. He had been uncovered in 1928 and ejected from the party. An ex-Mountie in California had told a former resident of Regina about Leopold arriving in the barracks one day and departing as Esselwein. The man told a visiting friend from his home town who was a Communist and the information got back to Canada. Leopold's testimony resulted in eight leaders of the Communist Party going to jail.

Vernon Kemp's career during the 1920s shows another dimension of the Force. He became a fully-fledged member of the Force in 1915, and rose to Sergeant a year and a half later. He served in France for a brief spell, and returned to be promoted to inspector at the age of 25 in 1920. He became second-in-command of 'A' Division, the only real Mountie in what had been the Dominion Police. These police dressed like British bobbies, and guarded

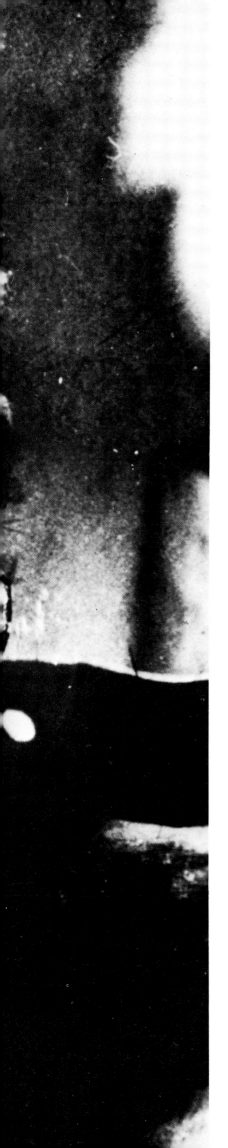

Chapter 12

THE MAD TRAPPER, ROSE MARIE AND ROUTINE WORK

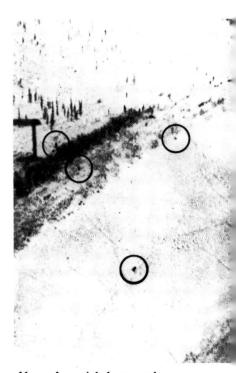

Above: An aerial photograph of the scene on Eagle River where Albert Johnson made his last stand. Members of the Force hid behind the trees.
Opposite: The death photo of Albert Johnson, the Mad Trapper.

When the Conservatives under R B Bennett came to power in August 1930, the Force's fortunes changed dramatically. The new Prime Minister, a Calgary lawyer well aware of the work of the Mounties, decided to give them proper backing and support. But the Force again had to maintain order during riots and strikes. 'Jimmy' Starnes retired after 45 years of service just after the new government took office. Bennett persuaded Major General James MacBrien to become Commissioner in 1931. He had enlisted as a constable in 1900, left the Force to serve in the Boer War, and rose from private to general in the Canadian Army, retiring as the Chief of its General Staff. A qualified pilot, Sir James, as he later became, was general manager and director of Canadian Airways.

A famous incident in the winter of 1931-32 convinced the Force, the politicians and others, of the value of aeroplanes for police work. On 9 July 1931, a man floated down the Peel River on a raft and landed at Fort McPherson. The police in the North always kept their eye on newcomers and something must have struck them about this man who had no outfit, but plenty of money. Local traders from whom the man bought supplies reported that 'he comes in and gets what he wants and pays for it and bothers no one.' Constable Millen sought out the man. He spoke with a faint Scandinavian accent, gave his name as Albert Johnson, and answered questions in an evasive manner. No one ever learned the true identity of the man who became known as 'The Mad Trapper of Rat

River.' He wanted to cross the mountains into the Yukon, and Millen cautioned him that if he wanted to trap, he'd have to obtain a license.

The Force had a fair amount of experience with eccentrics and madmen in the North; part of their duty consisted of accompanying them outside. 'Crazy' Smith on Sulphur Creek in the Yukon had been considered harmless and eccentric until he burst from his cabin in January 1926 and threatened a passer-by. Mounties tried to take him into custody, but Smith barricaded himself in his cabin, and fired at anyone who approached. Eventually he was killed by a ricocheting bullet.

Albert Johnson vanished into the wild country west of the Mackenzie. Around Christmas, an Indian reported that someone had destroyed his traps in the Rat River country. Constable King and Special Constable Joseph Bernard found Johnson's cabin 72 miles west of Arctic Red River, but no one replied to their greeting. They went back to Aklavik to obtain a search warrant, and returned with more men on New Year's Eve. This time the patrol was greeted with a rifle shot that wounded King. Another party then set out to arrest Johnson who had turned his cabin into a log fortress. Not even dynamite could dislodge him, so the patrol retreated. When Millen and a trapper returned to the cabin in mid-January, it was empty, but they traced Johnson, who killed the constable in a shoot-out.

Wind and snow wiped out Johnson's tracks as he headed across the empty land. The Force hired a Canadian Airways Bellanca piloted by Captain W R 'Wop' May, to supply the next patrol and to find Johnson. In mid-February, May picked up the Mad Trapper's tracks on the Bell River in the Yukon, and patrols followed him down that river and up the Eagle, catching him on February 17. In the final shoot-out, Johnson shot one pursuer through the lung, and ten minutes later he lay dead. Johnson had two rifles and a shot gun, gold dust, $2410 in cash – but no identification. Wop May flew the wounded man back to hospital in Aklavik in 50 minutes, saving his life.

Through the 1930s, MacBrien worked hard to help the Force regain lost ground and to introduce modern methods of crime detection. In 1932, the Mounties took over from the provincial police in Alberta, Manitoba, New Brunswick, Nova Scotia and Prince Edward Island; Saskatchewan had returned to the fold in 1928. The Mounties absorbed the members of the provincial police forces, and extended policing to municipalities, starting with Flin Flon, Manitoba, in 1935. Many communities could not afford their own police forces as the Depression bit into their budgets, and they contracted with the RCMP for their services. Thus Mounties had to undertake the boring and monotonous tasks formerly done by untrained men who also acted as firemen, dog catchers and town hall janitors. They left behind them, however, a legacy of efficient and honest policing.

In 1933, the Force established a museum at Regina, and started publication of the *Quarterly*. Four years later they picked up the idea of a Modus Operandi section on criminals from New Scotland Yard; this classified law-

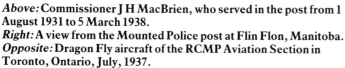

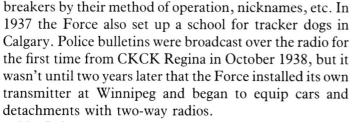

Above: Commissioner J H MacBrien, who served in the post from 1 August 1931 to 5 March 1938.
Right: A view from the Mounted Police post at Flin Flon, Manitoba.
Opposite: Dragon Fly aircraft of the RCMP Aviation Section in Toronto, Ontario, July, 1937.

breakers by their method of operation, nicknames, etc. In 1937 the Force also set up a school for tracker dogs in Calgary. Police bulletins were broadcast over the radio for the first time from CKCK Regina in October 1938, but it wasn't until two years later that the Force installed its own transmitter at Winnipeg and began to equip cars and detachments with two-way radios.

MacBrien overhauled recruit training, moving the emphasis from drill and discipline to courses reflecting the increasing complexity of police work. Horse patrols phased out in the 1930s, and in 1937 a modern crime detection laboratory opened at Regina. Two years later another one opened at Rockcliffe in the Ottawa area.

In 1936, the Commissioner flew his own plane on an 11,000 mile tour of the Force, spending only five days on the ground. In the following year he created the 'Air' Division with four deHavilland Dragonfly planes and nine men. It soon proved its worth in a wide range of police activities.

Sir James died in office in 1938, but he left behind an impressive legacy. By 1939, with a total establishment of just over 2600, the RCMP had become one of the world's top police forces. And Hollywood had glamourized and distorted its style of operation beyond belief. The Force co-operated with the film makers in the hope that they would show it in a favourable light. They did – but the Mounties always emerged looking like Western sheriffs.

Hollywood garbed them in a strange variety of costumes, and had problems in providing the right sort of headgear. In *River's End* and *McKenna of the Mounted* a dishonourably discharged Mountie has to run the gauntlet of fellow officers who lash him with belts. In *Yukon Manhunt*, Kirby Grant paddles a birchbark canoe – in full Review Order uniform. These films propagated the myth that a Mountie who does not get his man has to resign from the Force, and that the RCMP motto is 'We always get our man' rather than *Maintiens Le Droit* – 'Uphold the Right.'

The ultimate Mountie movie, *Rose Marie*, appeared in 1936 and starred Nelson Eddie and Jeanette MacDonald. In it the Mounties sang their way through the north woods as they rode after wicked men. Commissioner MacBrien and his staff liked the film when first they saw it, but it became a cross to the Force. Posts with light work loads earned the label 'Rose Marie Detachments' and good looking fellow officers imbued with a sense of their own importance were called 'Nelson Eddies.'

Rose Marie, a smash hit, inspired other Mountie movies, including *Susannah of the Mounties* starring Shirley Temple in 1939.

North West Mounted Police, launched with loads of hype in Regina in 1940, made a travesty of the Force's history and maligned the Métis who always seemed to end up as the villains in Mountie movies. The movie claimed to tell the story of the 1885 Riel Rebellion, and showed 50

Mounties, including their commanding officer, being mown down by a Gatling gun at Duck Lake. Producer Cecil B De Mille gave the gun to the Métis to increase the odds against the Mounties, and hence to enhance their stature as heroes. A recent book lumps all Mountie movies into the category of 'Western Movies' and says of *North West Mounted Police*: 'A Texas Ranger pursues a fugitive to Canada; beyond that, the plot is impossible to follow.' But, the writer added, 'De Mille's first Technicolor epic is worth seeing mainly for the Mounties' red coats that brighten the screen.'

Mountie life in the Thirties bore little resemblance to the screen version. The human dimensions of police work changed little, nor did living conditions improve. In provincial detachments, the Force tried to save money by billeting single men in the spare room in married quarters. Many posts had no plumbing or running water inside. Drunks in the cells that formed part of the living quarters howled and cursed all night, keeping the policemen's wives and children awake. And in the morning, they expected breakfast.

During the Depression, officers dispensed relief and reported to the government on the conditions among the unemployed. An unknown Mountie writing from Alberta in 1932 noted that 'While the relief line continues in operation there is very little crime . . .' But by mid-summer, eight men had already been committed to Ponoka Mental Asylum – 'none of these cases have been violent.' The Mountie accompanied a doctor to interview a married man 'on complaint of the wife, that she thought her husband mentally sick.' He had threatened to shoot her 'if economic conditions and his own status did not change.' The Mountie deplored the relief system which was 'underminding' [sic] people and making them 'lazy, dissatisfied' and encouraging them to 'socialistic ideas.'

On Dominion Day in 1932, steel-helmeted Mounties battled 3000 relief camp residents and sympathizers in Regina during the 'On To Ottawa' trek of the unemployed. The rioters beat a city detective to death and injured five Mounties who fired shots to disperse the crowds, wounding one man. In the next year, Inspector Lorne Sampson died after falling from his horse while trying to suppress a disturbance in Saskatoon. In October 1935, three Doukhobor robbery suspects shot Constable Shaw near Pelly, Saskatchewan, and then killed Sergeant Wallace near Banff, Alberta.

An insight into life in the prairie detachments comes from Max Braithwaite's *The Night We Stole the Mountie's Car*. Braithwaite, a school teacher during the Depression, set out to write an angry book, but it turned into a humorous one. The Mounties, he writes, were 'respected, revered, feared or detested,' depending on your point of view. One, a Ukrainian, got along with everyone. Another, a Scot, who had served in the Arctic, liked to knit. Braithwaite got some good stories from him about his work in the North, and sent them off for publication. They were rejected by editors because they did not fit the image of gallant Mounties galloping over the plains in hot

pursuit of Indians. The Scot finally caught a bootlegger with a bottle of his vile-smelling brew. The man smashed the bottle against the Mountie's tunic to destroy the evidence. The policeman whipped off the coat, and squeezed the brew into a glass to obtain enough liquor for a conviction. But he never did get rid of the smell of the homebrew on his tunic. A third Mountie, an Englishman, set local people's teeth on edge. Cultured and superior, he saw his role as civilizing the colonials. He enthralled women with tales of adventures throughout the Empire, organized a tennis club and beat everyone at the game.

But he lacked a sense of humour, as Braithwaite and a friend discovered when they borrowed his car after an evening of drinking. The Mountie threw them in jail, but

the Sergeant in charge of the detachment released them the next morning. This officer, a 'good, tough Saskatchewan guy' was 'the kind you could trust,' concluded Braithwaite.

War broke out as Mountie movies made the rounds of theatres. Suddenly the laughter died as the Force went onto a war footing. Commissioner Stuart Taylor Wood, a descendant of President Zachary Taylor, had become the eighth head of the Force, a position he held until 1951. After him, seven commissioners would hold office in the period up to 1977 – just one sign of the loss of innocence that Canadians suffered during the war and post-war years as established organizations strove to cope with growth and change.

Top left: A photo of the Regina Riot – 1 July 1935. This occurred in Market Square and was a confrontation between transient unemployed and some citizens of Regina, and it was broken up by police.
Top: Unemployed people demonstrating at the Parliament Building in Edmonton, Alberta, in February 1929.
Above: Commissioner S T Wood, who served in that office from 6 March 1938 to 30 April 1951.

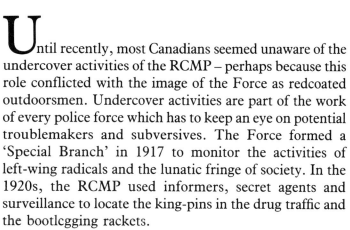

Chapter 13
SUBVERSIVES AND SPIES

Until recently, most Canadians seemed unaware of the undercover activities of the RCMP – perhaps because this role conflicted with the image of the Force as redcoated outdoorsmen. Undercover activities are part of the work of every police force which has to keep an eye on potential troublemakers and subversives. The Force formed a 'Special Branch' in 1917 to monitor the activities of left-wing radicals and the lunatic fringe of society. In the 1920s, the RCMP used informers, secret agents and surveillance to locate the king-pins in the drug traffic and the bootlegging rackets.

The success of covert activities depends on the ability of individual officers to discriminate between harmless eccentrics and those willing to use force and violence to make their points. Some of the work of the RCMP before and during the Second World War illustrates the difficulty of this task.

In May 1939, King George VI and Queen Elizabeth crossed Canada by train, and the RCMP collected information on anyone who might disrupt the visit. A little old lady in northern Ontario claimed to be Queen Victoria, and visited Toronto to buy a new wardrobe and two oil paintings she planned to present to 'her children.' On the day the Royal Couple arrived in Québec, the woman parked herself in the royal enclosure – at the place where the King would inspect the Guard of Honour. The Mounties had kept her under surveillance, and an officer walked up to her, saluted, and asked her to move. 'Queen

Above: April 1937 – Commissioner J H MacBrien (left) and Assistant Commissioner S T Wood during the inspection of the Coronation Contingent prior to its departure for the coronation of King George VI.
Opposite: The *St Roch* in Dartmouth, Nova Scotia.

Victoria' graciously agreed to do so, and another Mountie officer told her story to a Lady-in-Waiting. She repeated it to the King and Queen who held a private audience for the little old lady, and accepted her paintings.

The Mounted Police had also kept the National Socialist Christian Party in Québec under surveillance: at one time its documents reached the Special Branch almost as quickly as they reached its leaders. The party, set up in 1934, had 12,000 members four years later. The Canadian Union of Fascists also came into being in the mid-30s, with branches in Winnipeg; Toronto; Woodstock, Ontario; Regina and Vancouver. The Force often had to keep order at Fascist meetings when leftwingers tried to break them up.

When Canada declared war on Germany on 10 September 1939, Canadians demanded that enemy aliens and Nazi sympathizers be jailed. The press whipped up fear of a 'fifth column.' When the German armies moved into action in the spring of 1940 and overran Denmark, Norway, the Netherlands, Belgium and northern France, the British arrested Sir Oswald Mosely and members of the British Union of Fascists. The RCMP raided Arcand's headquarters in Montréal, and removed truckloads of swastika banners, maps, membership lists and anti-Semitic literature from Germany. Arcand and ten members of the organization were captured, tried and interned at Fredericton, New Brunswick. In all, about two hundred alleged Nazis were rounded up in this important foray.

The Force also arrested about 100 left-wing and labour activitists. The Communist Party of Canada had been declared illegal in 1940, but its leaders went underground and urged students not to volunteer to serve in a 'capitalistic and imperialistic war.' In December 1940 an illegal radio station, claiming to be 'the voice of Canada,' began spewing out Communist propaganda. A month later, Constable Mascall arrested Allan Beswick Parsons, a skiing enthusiast who took off frequently for the hills around Toronto. His Chrysler, equipped with a transmitter with a 2000 mile range, had served as the ɔbile base for his anti-war efforts. Most of the Communists and left-wingers gave their support to Canada's war effort in June 1941, when Germany invaded Russia and the conflict suddenly became a fight for freedom and democracy. They were released from the detention camps.

A year earlier, when Italy declared war on the Allies, the Mounties arrested 200 Fascists. The Nazis had given the 'Heil Hitler' routine to Mountie officers and only three of them identified themselves as non-Nazis. Only three of the Italians admitted to adhering to the Fascist cause – and they made excuses for doing so.

During the war, an RCMP officer received an offer from a group to send 5000 members into the highways and byways of the country to search for spies. The roundups the Mounties carried out initially had been unselective. The German nationals arrested at the beginning of the war were shipped to a camp in Kingston, Ontario. Here a tall,

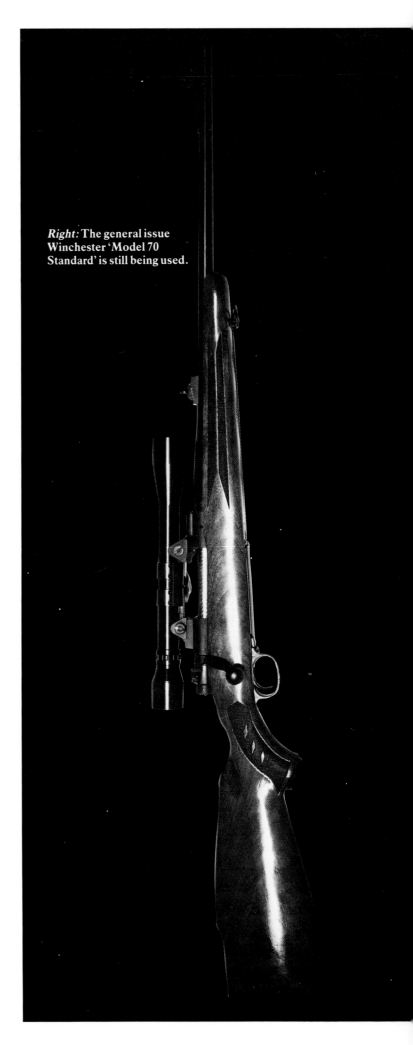

Right: The general issue Winchester 'Model 70 Standard' is still being used.

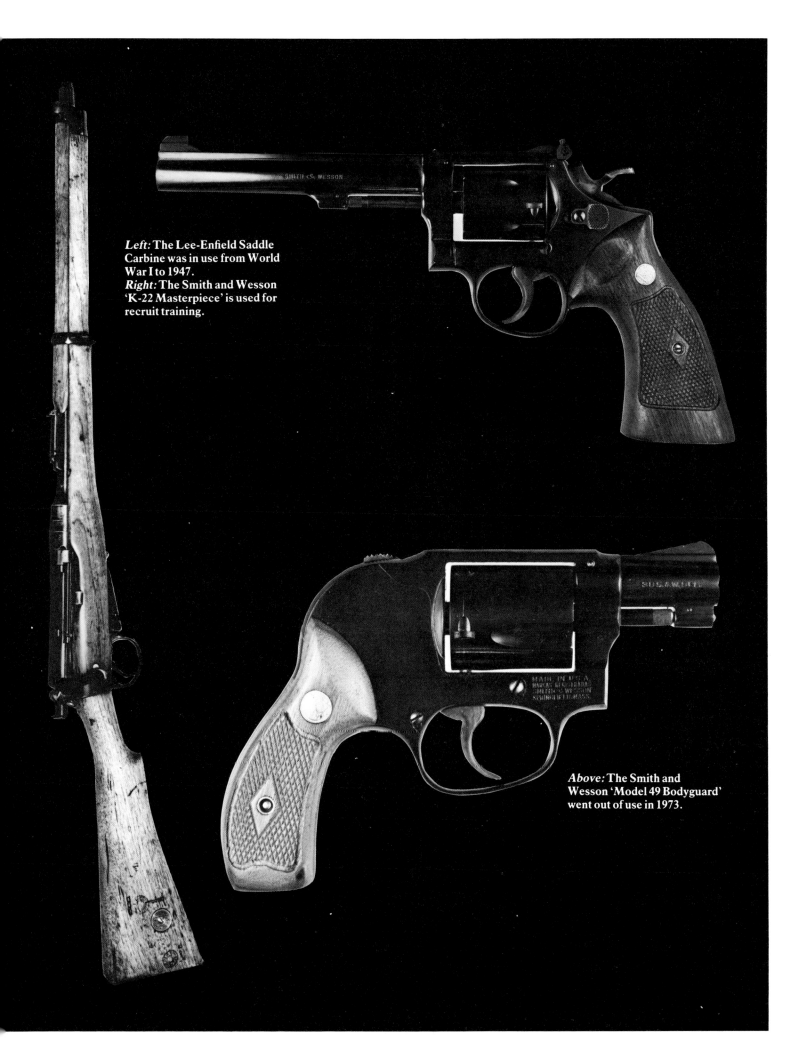

Left: The Lee-Enfield Saddle Carbine was in use from World War I to 1947.
Right: The Smith and Wesson 'K-22 Masterpiece' is used for recruit training.

Above: The Smith and Wesson 'Model 49 Bodyguard' went out of use in 1973.

blond, handsome leader arose who acted as spokesman, championing the cause of the prisoners. Camp authorities found him thoroughly obnoxious. His letters to his wife, filled with Biblical quotations and questions about their business, received replies telling him how terrible things were at home. Finally, his wife came to visit him on a wintry day. A frail creature, she walked the two miles from the railway station to the camp, and collapsed on arrival. When prisoners were moved to other camps, a number, including their blond leader, were released. He

was an RCMP undercover agent, sorting out the Nazis from the harmless internees.

When Rudolf Hess, Hitler's deputy, flew to Scotland in May 1941, rumours spread in Canada that he was held in Fort Henry, Kingston, Ontario, and mail began to arrive for him. One man wrote that he would be contacting Hess with an important message, and the Mounties went off to investigate him. He turned out to be a wino, living in a downtown flophouse, whose message turned out to be a screed of rambling nonsense. When the Mounties laughed

at it, the offended man said that he would contact Hess in another world.

Fear of the Japanese on the west coast triggered a shameful episode in Canada's history. Before the war, the RCMP had uncovered a smuggling ring that brought 2500 Japanese into Canada. None, however, was identified as a secret agent. Ottawa asked the Mounties to check the papers of Japanese in British Columbia in 1938, but out of 1881 individuals, only 11 were held for deportation. Early in 1941, the RCMP registered all Japanese in the west over the age of 16. When Japan attacked Pearl Harbor and Hong Kong on 7 December 1941, the Federal Government ordered the arrest of 38 Japanese considered a threat to national security and impounded 1200 boats owned by native and foreign-born Japanese.

Despite assurances from the RCMP that the few potentially dangerous Japanese had been interned, some politicians forced the Federal and British Columbia governments into a mass evacuation of all Japanese from the coast. The RCMP had to round up 21,000 Japanese

and move them inland; they encountered little resistance. The Force provided detachments to guard the camps, and were made responsible for security around them.

Before war began, the Mounties had surveyed industrial plants, harbours, canals and other key sites, and advised government and industry on their security. As war approached, the RCMP began to guard vital installations, stretching its manpower very thin. One NCO married on a Saturday – and was back at his desk on the Sunday. The Force created a special reserve, many of whom were prominent businessmen. During the war, the RCMP's strength rose to 4743, including 1506 special constable guards.

On the outbreak of war, 215 members had taken leave of absence and joined the army. Another 150 members of the Marine Division went into the Royal Canadian Navy. They were some of the few trained seamen the country possessed. 'Seamen?' one naval official remarked early in the war. 'I have no seamen except the "Mounties" and the "Rummies" they used to chase.' Forty members of the Air Division joined the Royal Canadian Air Force. The RCMP boats and aircraft – except for one Norseman aircraft kept for use in the North – became part of Canada's armed forces. Many of the Mounties formed the Provost Company of the First Candian Division, serving on the Dieppe Raid, in Italy and Northwest Europe. About 150 Mounties secured commissions, and the Force's Honour Roll lists 14 members who died in action, mainly in Italy.

At home, the Mounties cracked a case involving the smuggling of gold from Northern Ontario, and investigated tax frauds, black market operations and ration coupon theft and forging. They were also asked to ensure that tea cups were not produced with handles and that sliced bread was not sold in stores. The government forbade such wasteful practices but the Force wasted little time tracking down offenders in these fields. They had also to search for deserters from the Armed Forces, and this task became difficult in 1945 when the government ordered conscripts to serve in Europe. In one case, the investigators learned that two brothers, both deserters, had drowned. Impressed with the grief displayed by the relatives, the Mounties closed the file. A few weeks later, the US Immigration Service handed over the two 'deceased' who had been trying to move south of the border after their demise.

During the war, the Mounties became involved in searching for spies. In November 1942, a German landed from a submarine at New Carlisle on Chaleur Bay. Two Mounties, and Johnny, a special constable, went down to interrogate him. Johnny had been a submariner during World War One, then risen to become a leader of the German Communist Party, fleeing to Moscow after Hitler came to power. Here he trained saboteurs until becoming disenchanted with Russian Communism. He offered his services to British Intelligence who had used him until his cover had been blown on an assignment in South America. The Force had provided asylum for him in Canada.

The German who had arrived by sea had lived in Canada before the war, and paid bills with notes withdrawn from circulation in the country. He even had an incorrect registration certificate. When arrested, he claimed to be a naval officer who had deserted and demanded that he be allowed to dig up the uniform he had buried on the beach and wear it. When the Mounties arrived, they told him to change back into civilian clothes. The man clicked his heels, bowed and demanded that he be treated as an officer and a gentleman. The Mountie officer replied, 'Nuts. Sit down and keep quiet until I speak to you.'

The Mounties 'turned' the spy, after draining every scrap of information from him. They set up a transmitter in Johnny's house in Montréal and the spy contacted Hamburg. The Germans asked a lot of questions about Canada, but never sent any hard information on their plans. So Johnny, playing the role of a Nazi agent, infiltrated the remnants of the Fascist party in Québec which was plotting sabotage. He kept them under tight control, then set up a meeting at Montréal's Windsor Hotel with a German spy who had also been turned. He harangued the Fascists and convinced them of the futility of their ideas of sabotage.

Another spy reached New Brunswick, moved to Montréal and was arrested in a raid on a brothel there. Claiming to be a married man, he paid a fine, and then escaped to Ottawa. Here he stayed in a rooming house and spent his days watching movies, playing pool and listening to Parliamentary debates in the visitors' gallery of the House of Commons. His funds ran out after a year so the spy simply walked into the RCMP headquarters in Ottawa and surrendered.

The equipment used by the spy who came ashore near New Carlisle can be seen in the RCMP Museum in Regina; it includes a copy of *Mary Poppins* for the preparation of code messages.

This spy had been a former French Foreign Legionnaire, who claimed that he had been forced into spying. Some other German Legionnaires had been drafted into the army and captured in North Africa. In the prisoner-of-war camp at Medicine Hat, Alberta, these men kept to themselves, and were 'tried' by the hard-core Nazis who ran the camp because they were luke-warm to their cause. On 22 June 1943, a mob lynched one of the Legionnaires. Corporal Bull worked on this case until October 1945, when he had enough evidence to make some arrests. While this investigation took place, a former professor of languages and an outspoken anti-Nazi in the camp, was lured into a hut, beaten, gagged and hung from a pipe in such a way as to suggest suicide. Corporal Bull also handled this case, securing confessions from the men responsible. They went to the gallows in Lethbridge, Alberta, in December 1946. One of their RCMP guards had cut down the body of the murdered language professor. But as he remarked, 'While guarding the prisoners, we became quite attached to them.' One shined his boots because 'he didn't want to go into court with a scruffy-looking policeman.'

Sergeant H A Larsen in Arctic
Dress – 1943.

Some prisoners of war managed to escape, and the Force was called in to capture them. But on one occasion, they refused to thwart a mass break-out. Coded messages had been sent to a camp which housed seven of Germany's leading submarine experts. An escape was planned so that these men could reach the shores of New Brunswick, to be picked up by a submarine. Naval Intelligence did not know the location of the pick-up point and wanted to nab the submarine. So the Mounties staked out the camp, with instructions to allow the escape. The prisoners dug a tunnel as the Mounties kept watch, bitten by mosquitoes and soaked by autumn rains. Finally three men broke out, and were interrogated. They proved to have escaped with-out the permission of the camp's official escape committee. This abortive attempt must have discouraged the prisoners of war, or the German officers received orders to discontinue their efforts to escape. Tunnelling stopped.

Just after the war ended, a cipher clerk in the Russian embassy in Ottawa defected, and revealed the existence of a Soviet espionage network to the RCMP.

The Gouzenko case plunged the Force into the murky waters of a post-war world where diplomatic negotiations between nations were complemented with espionage and terrorism by small groups of fanatics who merged with the general population and usually were indistinguishable from ordinary people – until they acted.

Chapter 14

HANDLING POST-WAR TENSIONS

The Russians treat espionage as part of their foreign policy, and staff members at their embassies abroad are members of the KGB, the Commission of State Security. Canada has a military intelligence group abroad which keeps a very low profile. Since Canada, as a member of NATO and other western alliances, has access to secret information of interest to the Russians, they have paid some attention to recruiting spies and informants.

When Igor Gouzenko arrived in Canada in 1943 as a cipher clerk at the Russian embassy in Ottawa, the range of food and consumer goods and the freedom enjoyed by Canadians amazed him. He learned that the Russians were gathering information on Canada's nuclear projects at Chalk River, Ontario. Just before he was due to return home, Gouzenko took a number of documents from the embassy and defected with his family in September 1945. He failed to interest an Ottawa newspaper in his story. One reporter told him that nobody 'wants to say anything but nice things about Stalin these days.' Gouzenko tried to see the Minister of Justice, Louis St Laurent, without success. When his colleagues came in search of him, Gouzenko turned for help to a neighbour, a sergeant in the RCAF. He cycled off to fetch the Ottawa police who put Gouzenko under protective surveillance and then brought in the RCMP. The defection terrified Prime Minister Mackenzie King who feared it might upset the Russians. Five months after Gouzenko left the Soviet Embassy, no arrests had been made based on the information about the

Above: A RCMP Dogmaster and his police service dog – 1949.
Opposite: The VE Day riots in Halifax, Nova Scotia, 8 May 1945. This is Hollis Street looking south from the Salter and Hollis intersection.

The Royal Canadian Mounted Police 'Musical Ride' perform the 'Wagon Wheel' formation.

Right: Two members of the Force beside their plane, a Norseman CF-MPL, at Edmonton, Alberta, in March 1950.

Below: A member of the Royal Canadian Mounted Police issuing rations to Eskimo native special constables at Pond Inlet Detachment, 1951.

Below: A Royal Canadian Mounted Policeman baking bread at the Pond Inlet Detachment – 1951.

spy rings that he provided. Nor had anything been made public about the Russian quest for Canada's atomic secrets. Nine people were eventually convicted of spying for the Russians, including Fred Rose, a member of Parliament.

The Force began to put together a security section. After the Russian embassy in Ottawa burned down on New Year's Day, 1956, the RCMP bugged the new building. The new security section contained some civilians, and the Force trained some Mounties in surveillance techniques. As one individual put it, however, 'The Russians used to spot us immediately and wave at us.' The security section undertook a number of operations, including 'Keystone,' 'Dew Worm,' 'Apple Cider' and 'Moby Dick,' involving Russian agents and double agents. But the Russians did not seem very interested in what was happening in Canada. One operation involved George Victor Spencer, a Vancouver postal clerk ejected from the Communist Party of Canada, who gathered information on pipelines in the west and passed it on to Russian contacts. This lonely man became the subject of a special government commission which reported in 1966.

The Royal Canadian Mounted Police Musical Ride perform the 'Four Circle' formation.

In the same year another commission enquired into 'Matters Relating to One Gerda Munsinger.' The lady in question, a German prostitute, petty thief and smuggler who had spied for the Russians, had an intimate relationship with a key member of Prime Minister John Diefenbaker's cabinet. Three years later, yet another Royal Commission examined National Security and recommended that a separate civilian agency be formed to take care of it.

The Force clung to its role in this field, although it appointed a civilian Director-General of the Security Service in 1970, but he was replaced by a former general three years later. During the 1970s, the strains of social

change and especially the upsurge of nationalism in Québec led to increasing stress on security activities. Some Mounties overstepped the law and showed too much initiative in searching for subversives. As one member of the Force put it, 'I wasn't exactly consulting my Boy Scout Manual on how I was going to approach someone.' The burning of a barn to prevent a clandestine meeting, breakins of offices, and the theft of the Parti Québécoise's mailing list during the 1970s revealed that the Security Service had developed a 'dirty tricks' section that forms part of all national intelligence operations. When information about these excesses leaked out, two Royal Commissions examined RCMP wrongdoings. The federal

Opposite Sergeant Reid (left) and Sergeant Cormier of the Royal Canadian Mounted Police Air Services, with their CF-FHW Beaver at Vancouver, British Columbia, 1952.
Right: A member of the Eastern Arctic Patrol insepecting pelts – 1957.
Below: RCMP member inspecting pelts – another photo from the Eastern Arctic Patrol.

Above: A Royal Canadian Mounted Police aircraft and a dog team at Fort Reliance, North West Territories, 1958.
Below: A Royal Canadian Mounted Police dog team at White Horse, Yukon Territory, 1965.

Above: A photograph of the issue revolvers of the Force – 1963.
Right: A capture of an escape from the Brannen Lake School in British Columbia in 1965.

McDonald Commission started its enquiry in the summer of 1977, and reported four years later. In Québec, the provincial government set up the Keable Commission at the same time, and it ran until February 1979.

The revelations of these two commissions alarmed many Canadians, and also crippled Canada's security operations. In 1965-66, the Federal Government moved the RCMP from the Department of Justice to the new portfolio of Solicitor-General, which was also responsible for penitentiaries and the parole system. When W L Higgitt became Commissioner in 1969, he warned Prime Minister Trudeau that his policy of fostering closer links with mainland China and the opening of a Chinese Embassy in Ottawa would endanger national security. Higgitt had worked on the Gouzenko case, and been promoted for his intelligence work. His advice angered Trudeau, who said that the new commissioner was 'allowed one mistake.'

Effective intelligence work rests on suspicion, and it is based on two principles – 'need to know' and 'deniability.' The latter is a polite name for lying and the former ensures that no one individual knows what is going on in the whole system, but gets just enough information to do his or her job. These principles contradict those that underlie effective police work in modern society, which depends on a broad understanding of social change and the co-operation of the public.

C Starnes, 1923-1931

L H Nicholson, 1951-1959

C E Rivett-Carnac, 1959-1960

C O M M I S S I O N E R S

1. Lt. Col. W. Osborne SMITH (Temporary) — September 25, 1973 – October 17, 1873
2. Commissioner George Arthur FRENCH — October 18, 1873 – July 21, 1876
3. Commissioner James Farquharson MACLEOD, C.M.G. — July 22, 1876 – October 31, 1880
4. Commissioner Acheson Gosford IRVINE — November 1, 1880 – March 31, 1896
5. Commissioner Lawrence William HERCHMER — April 1, 1886 – July 31, 1900
6. Commissioner Aylesworth Bowen PERRY, C.M.G. — August 1, 1900 – March 31, 1923
7. Commissioner Cortlandt STARNES — April 1, 1923 – July 31, 1931
8. Commissioner Sir James Howden MacBRIEN, K.C.B. C.M.G., D.S.O. — August 1, 1931 – March 5, 1938
9. Commissioner Stuart Taylor WOOD, C.M.G. — March 6, 1938 – April 30, 1951
10. Commissioner Leonard Manson NICHOLSON M.B.E. — May 1, 1951 – March 31, 1959
11. Commissioner Charles Edward RIVETT-CARNAC — April 1, 1959 – March 31, 1960
12. Commissioner Clifford Walter HARVISON — April 1, 1960 – October 31, 1963
13. Commissioner George Brinton McCLELLAN — November 1, 1963 – August 14, 1967
14. Commissioner Malcolm Francis Aylesworth LINDSAY — August 15, 1967 – September 30, 1969
15. Commissioner William Leonard HIGGITT — October 1, 1969 – December 20, 1973
16. Commissioner Maurice Jean NADON — January 1, 1974 – August 31, 1977
(Acting Commissioner December 29-31, 1973)

W L Higgitt, 1969-1973

M J Nadon, 1974-1977

R H Simmonds 1977

C W Harvison, 1960-1963   G B McClelland, 1963-1967   M F A Lindsay, 1967-1969

The difficulties experienced by the Force as it tried to come to terms with a time of rapid change illustrate the problems old organizations have in handling ambiguity.

Even in 1942, the Force had 600 cars – and only 125 horses. Yet the horseman mentality still pervaded its upper ranks. Commissioner Woods proclaimed in 1949 that 'There's nothing like a horse for finding out the weak spots in a man,' and claimed that the riding school was the proving ground of the Force.

The RCMP made valiant efforts in the post-war years to improve its image and to generate public support. The Musical Ride, begun in 1904 as a form of public entertainment, travelled throughout Canada after its revival in 1948. By the time this splendid display of discipline and horsemanship appeared at Expo '70 in Osaka, Japan, equitation (the care and management of horses) had disappeared from the Force's training programme. The RCMP band also went on tour for the first time in 1948, and the Force launched a campaign to inform young people about its work and to deter them from careers in crime.

The RCMP also continued its routine work throughout Canada. In a small town in Alberta the Force was called in to investigate the robbery of a piggy bank in September, 1951. The investigating officer sensed something amiss, and uncovered a bomb in the bed of the owner of the piggy bank. The robbery had been used to cover up a plot by a jilted suitor. When Newfoundland entered Confederation on 1 April 1949, the RCMP became responsible for enforcing federal laws there, and 16 months later took over provincial policing. On 15 August 1950, the Force became responsible for policing British Columbia.

Post-war affluence created new policing problems. As more Canadians obtained cars, highway patrols increased. In Alberta, 16 patrol cars travelled a million miles on traffic duties in 1953-54. Counterfeiting, cigarette smuggling (one shipment moved from Detroit to Windsor in a coffin), fraud and the rise of the drug traffic and of organized crime stretched the Force's resources.

A couple of years after the war ended, Le Marquis Joseph Charles Gouin de Fontenailles arrived in Joliette, Québec, announcing plans to build factories to produce waterproof cement blocks. The business leaders gave this

Commissioner L H Nicholson, who served from 1951-1959.

man unlimited credit. Despite his shabby clothes, he exuded confidence. When the police investigated the marquis, they reported that he was a con man, a former Montréal potwasher.

The Force unmasked another swindler in Winnipeg in 1953. He persuaded people to invest in his inventions, including a radioactive flashlight and a device for turning water into gasoline. In the following year, the RCMP began to investigate the activities of Dr Alfred Valdamis, a Lithuanian brought to Newfoundland by Premier Smallwood to generate economic development. This man had been taking a cut from the contracts for the new projects he helped to establish in the province.

The Mounties remained the 'available men' during the 1950s, but other government agencies expanded their

activities into areas they once considered their domain. When the Department of Northern Affairs and National Resources came into being in 1954, it sent northern service officers into Inuit settlements to do work once done by the Mounties. Henry Larsen wrote of the publicity surrounding this new department, 'much of it centred on the sins of omission and commission of the past.' Those who had 'never given a single thought to the plight of the Eskimos' were now 'setting themselves up as some kind of guilty conscience' and blaming others for the problems in the North.

By March 1954, the Force numbered 6222, including 4420 members in uniform. The RCMP had acquired a new headquarters building in Ottawa in the previous year, a former seminary on what was then the outskirts of the city. Contracting in certain areas and expanding in others, the Force found itself caught in the crossfire between the Conservative Government in Ottawa and the Newfoundland Liberals under Joseph Smallwood when a labour war broke out in the woods in 1959.

Above: **A crew member of the Royal Canadian Mounted Police vessel** *MacBrien* **fires a line to aid a sinking American trawler, 1948.**

Under their contracts with provincial governments, the Force can provide extra officers in an emergency – if help is requested by the provincial attorney-general and approved by the Federal Government. When the International Woodworkers of America tried to organize loggers and others in Newfoundland, Premier Smallwood founded a rival union, and violence erupted. The officer commanding 'B' Division asked the federal Minister of Justice to send reinforcements. A cabinet minister told Commissioner Nicholson, 'I'm damned if we'll pull their political chestnuts out of the fire.' The Federal Government refused to send more RCMP officers and Nicholson resigned.

The Force steadily modernized its operations and established links with international organizations. It joined Interpol in 1949, and Commissioner Higgitt became President of this international crimefighting body in 1972. In 1950, sled patrols covered 46,860 miles. Nearly 20 years later, in March 1969, the last dog patrol left Old Crow in the Yukon, visited Arctic Red River, and re-

Right: Service order of dress Number 2, 1960.
Left: Crew members aboard the RCMP vessel *MacBrien* prepare for the rescue of the American trawler *Bonnie*, March 1948.

turned to base after travelling 500 miles in 16 days. The Force now uses snow toboggans in the northern winters. The first postwar crime laboratory opened in Sackville, New Brunswick, in 1958 and others started operating in Vancouver (1963), Edmonton (1968), Winnipeg (1973) and Halifax (1979). The Canadian Police Information Centre, a computerized system, began operations in 1967, putting information on stolen cars, wanted persons and other matters at the fingertips of every Mountie in Canada.

In the late 1960s, two Mounties dressed as hippies penetrated the drug world in Montréal during an investigation that resulted in 27 people being charged with trafficking and possession. The sentiments of an older generation about change were summarized by a cartoon one member drew showing a bearded member of the counterculture on a government grant painting a peace symbol on the rump of a Mounted Policeman's horse. Frank Spalding, a gifted cartoonist who retired as Assistant Commissioner, produced a book entitled *100 years in the R.C.M.P. or, Stop the Musical Ride, I want Off!* in 1972. In it he complained that the 'RCMP along with *all* policemen, [are] being subjected to continuous outpourings of criticism mixed with vilification and abuse . . . never have so few . . . been criticized by so many.' To add to the Force's woes in a decade when the words 'freedom'

Above: A laboratory technician checks the Rh factor of a sample of blood found at the scene of a crime.
Left: Examining a semi-automatic weapon to find if any alterations have been done to its mechanism.
Right: Using an optical emission spectrograph to analyse metal fragments, powders and unknown materials.
Below: A fingerprint scanning computer.

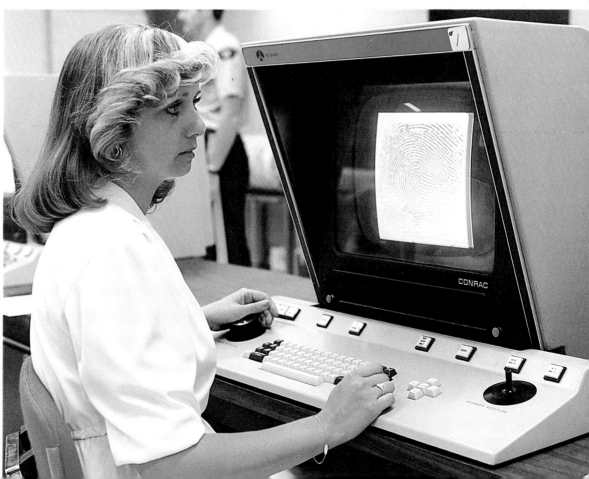

and 'liberation' became part of the current coin, a former member of the RCMP claimed in an article in *Maclean's* magazine of July 1972, that 'termites are gnawing at [the RCMP] tradition from within, weakening the whole structure.' Mounties even began to talk of unionizing.

At the beginning of the decade, the FLQ crisis jolted Canadians into an awareness of how law and order was handled in the peaceable kingdom. Cells of the Front de Libération de Québec kidnapped and killed a member of the provincial cabinet, and took a British Trade Commissioner prisoner. The Canadian Army had to be called in when the government invoked a state of 'apprehended insurrection.' Groping around in the dark, the police made 5000 raids, which netted 465 suspects of whom only 30 were convicted. During the next decade, the RCMP strengthened its surveillance of possible troublemakers and threats to society. In 1952-53, Doukhobors in British Columbia had again become restless and bombings of railways and power lines had taken place. Commissioner Nicholson pointed out the physical impossibility of patrolling every mile of railway track in the region.

In the late 1960s, Mounties searched through 250,000 passport applications and located one from James Earl Ray, the assassin of Martin Luther King, who had passed through Toronto on his way to Europe after killing the civil rights leader. The information about the passport helped police to capture Ray. When President Nixon visited Ottawa in 1971, Arthur Bremer stalked him with a rifle. So good was Mountie security that he never got a chance to fire. Later he shot and wounded Governor George Wallace of Alabama in the United States.

Numerous threats have been made against the life of Prime Minister Trudeau. The difficulties that Mounties face in evaluating such threats emerged in the case of one man found outside the Prime Minister's house with a .303-calibre rifle and a sawn-off baseball bat. One doctor described the man as a paranoid schizophrenic who had improved under treatment while another called him 'a flaming nut.'

Throughout its history, the Force has tried to stay clear of political meddling. But tensions within the RCMP grew as it struggled to change with the times, while neglecting to form mutually beneficial links with other federal agencies. The Force became a world unto itself. During the 1950s, one commanding officer forced security personnel to parade in full uniform. And when management consultants informed a commissioner that their recommendations would save the men an average of an hour a

day, he expressed delight: 'I've been looking for that hour to get the men out on parade!'

Robert Simmonds became Commissioner in 1977, taking over from Maurice Nadon, who had replaced Higgitt in 1974. The new commissioner had shown great skill in defusing an Indian incident in British Columbia through direct and honest dealings with the native peoples. Born in a small Saskatchewan community, Simmonds served as a pilot in the Fleet Air Arm of the Royal Navy during the Second World War, joined the Force in 1947, and rose through the ranks. He began to make the Force more accountable to the political system and to the general public. The Solicitor-General laid down guidelines to cover grey areas in security matters, and Department of Justice lawyers moved into RCMP headquarters to provide, on request, advice about the legality of investigative techniques.

After the McDonald Commission produced its report, the Federal Government began to establish a civilian security agency. The RCMP had accumulated files on 800,000 Canadians during the past two decades, relying on 'dangerous and unacceptable' definitions of subversion, according to the McDonald Commission. The government bill to create the Canadian Security Intelligence Service, nicknamed the 'Cissies,' came under immediate attack in Parliament and the media, for it seemed to give its members the power to break the law. Some commentators suggested that security remain with the RCMP, and the Senate established a Special Committee to study the bill.

Canada's new Constitution, adopted in 1982, contains a Charter of Rights and Freedoms to safeguard Canadians against arbitrary action by the police. The difficulties of future police work in areas like drug use were illustrated by a case in Nova Scotia in August 1983. The province's Supreme Court Appeal Division dismissed two Crown appeals on the ground that the RCMP violated the Charter when officers searched two men suspected of carrying narcotics. The two men involved had denied possession of drugs when interrogated by RCMP officers, who then searched them and found narcotics, and arrested them. The search was not deemed 'reasonable,' and the message that it wasn't what the police did, but how they did it, won't be ignored by the public.

Such stories illustrate the frustrations of police work in a rights-conscious society. But they also obscure the work of the RCMP in Canada and the reality of its day-to-day operations in preserving law and order.

Chapter 15

THE MODERN MOUNTIE

The Force graduated its first class of women recruits from the 'Depot' in Regina in 1974. In 1983, about 100 members of the RCMP graduated from universities, and the Force now recruits actively on campuses throughout Canada. In the past, men joined the Mounties for adventure or economic security – or because they had heard of their work. Now recruits join for the excellent pay and conditions, and for the opportunities for interesting work. The level of career satisfaction provided by the RCMP is indicated by the number of children of members who join the Force.

In June 1983, the total establishment of the Force numbered 16,955 members, including 564 officers, 13,155 NCOs, male and female constables, and 1432 special constables; the Force also employs 3629 public servants – their 'right arms,' as one officer put it. The annual budget for the RCMP is around $750 million, and one piece of its official literature likens it to a large corporation.

To become a Regular Member Constable, individuals must be Canadian citizens, aged 19 or over, physically and medically fit, able to drive a car, of good character and proficient in English or French. On joining up, the recruits go to the Training Academy at 'Depot' Division in Regina, and become members of a 32 person troop. The 25-week course includes academic subjects, instruction in self-defence, foot drill and small arms, and physical exercise. Discipline is strict, and a recruiting brochure

Above: Self defence training at Regina.
Opposite: Graduation ceremonies at the RCMP Academy at Regina.

Above: A pair of constables monitoring highway traffic.
Opposite: The RCMP Detachment at Pond Inlet, NWT.

states, 'The training environment at the Academy will probably be alien to you.' The training, however, does not appear to be any tougher than that for recruits in any military organization. Special constables undertake limited police duties, and their training lasts from 10 to 15 weeks.

When a recruit leaves the 'Depot,' he or she goes to a division, and is assigned to a training detachment. For six months the new Mountie is exposed to a wide range of police work; his or her progress is monitored by a divisional training supervisor. On completion of this internship period, the recruit becomes a fully-fledged operational policeman or policewoman.

The Force began to police Nova Scotia on 1 April 1932, and the work of 'H' Division there is typical of that of others, although the Atlantic Provinces have the lowest crime rate in Canada. The Division is broken up into sub-divisions and then into detachments. The establishment stands at 825 officers, men and civilians who staff 50 detachments and specialized units, some of which do work in the other Atlantic Provinces. Most policemen serve three to five years in the detachments before moving on to specialized fields. These cover gambling, commercial crime, drugs, illegal immigrants, police dogs, locksmiths, protection of federal property, telecommunications, field identification (forensic matters, fingerprints, photos), the administration of the Migratory Birds Act and other areas of concern.

The Commanding Officer of 'H' Division, Chief Superintendent Campbell Reid, a Cape Bretoner, joined the Force in 1953. He knew the reputation of the RCMP, liked to work with people, enjoyed travelling and wanted a career with an established organization. He has served in Corner Brook, Newfoundland; Labrador City; Penhold, Alberta and Ottawa, and was on his second tour in Nova Scotia in 1983.

'The role of the RCMP has not changed,' he says. 'We still prevent crime, preserve peace, and bring criminals to

Above; An RCMP migratory bird patrol checking a hunter's license.

Opposite top left: Foot drill at the Royal Canadian Mounted Police Academy – the 'Depot' – Regina, Saskatchewan, 1974.

Opposite top right: A Mountie and his guard dog.

Opposite bottom left: A member of the Force in winter dress in Northern Québec, 1962.

Left: A member of the Force performing airport security duty.

justice. The patterns of crime have not changed, but the techniques for their detection have become more sophisticated, commensurate with advances in science and technology. Crime detection remains based on investigation, interview, questions and leg work. Police work still rests on the accumulation of information.'

Some areas of crime are growing more quickly than others – white collar crime (stock and security frauds, fraudulent bankruptcies, land swindles, computer crime), the illicit use of drugs, and crimes rationalized by ideologies (bombings, hostage taking). The RCMP sent a member down to the Dutch Antilles when a company started swindling Haligonians with the sale of fraudulent sugar options. In July 1980, the drug squad seized four and a half tons of hashish on the *Sea Tern* near Peggy's Cove. As one member of the squad put it, 'It is a battle of wits. There is no vindictiveness.'

Above: Indian special constables
Opposite: The opening of Parliament in Ottawa, 18 October 1977 –
an RCMP escort for Queen Elizabeth II and Prince Philip.

As a national police force, the RCMP encompasses three political jurisdictions, can identify patterns of crime, bring together information quickly and concentrate a large number of resources if a crisis arises. Their computerized information system assists this process.

'We have the capability to respond to new trends in crime through specialized training and sophisticated equipment,' notes Reid. 'But we are also concerned with getting the police back in touch with the people in their communities. At one time, the police were the public and the public were the police, and there was a willingness by people to assist the police. Until recently, the public

abdicated this responsibility. They said, in effect, "We are paying you guys good money to handle crime – you do the work."'

The RCMP is changing this attitude with increased emphasis on preventive policing and community relations.

A woman hitch-hiker, raped by a motorist who picked her up, gave the RCMP an accurate description of the man's car. The local detachment contacted the media, and the community newspaper carried details of the rapist's car on its front page and within an hour the police had their man. In another part of Nova Scotia, a man took a bank teller hostage, forcing her to go with him to the bank on the next morning. An alert local individual sensed something unusual taking place, noted the license plate of a strange car, and passed it on to the police who caught the robber.

Under Option 3B, the force has been hiring and training Indians to police their reserves. They become Special Constables with access to the resources of the RCMP, and this method of policing has helped to establish rapport with native communities and to bridge the gap between the police and the people.

Also, Reid notes, 'there's more concern about the victims of crime these days – and rightly so.' He sees the emphasis on community work as a continuation of the historical tradition of the RCMP. 'The policeman is not just the guy who stands at the corner or chases thieves. He's an integral part of the community.'

This role has become easier to play in recent years because the Force does not transfer its officers as often as it once did. Single men could spend as little as six months in one detachment, and married men two years.

Superintendent Cal Bungay, Officer Commanding the Halifax Sub-Division, came from a 'family with few means' in North Sydney. Local members of the RCMP ate at the house of a local lady and he 'admired them from a distance.' His father had been a soldier, and Bungay was active in cadets. He joined the Force in 1952 and served in Saskatchewan, Prince Edward Island and Newfoundland before arriving in Nova Scotia in 1975. With a staff of 243, the Halifax Sub-Division covers most of central Nova Scotia, excluding the cities of Halifax and Dartmouth and the town of Bedford.

Crime seems to be levelling off in the province. Casual criminals are less mobile because of the high cost of gas

Above: An RCMP vessel and helicopter on patrol.
Above, inset: The RCMP *McClellan* on patrol.
Right center: An RCMP 'Otter' aircraft.
Bottom right: Snowmobile patrol, Cartwright, Labrador.
Opposite: A member of the Force at Lake Louise, Banff, Alberta.
Below: The RCMP patrol vessel *Tofino* Near Prince Rupert, BC.

and of motor vehicles. 'Professional criminals, of course, will steal them if they are in need. But others are not running the roads as much as they did, on the lookout for cars to strip,' notes Bungay.

The increasing emphasis on crime prevention has also had an impact. 'Our high visibility on the roads helps to establish good relations with the public; 99% of the contact the public has with the RCMP is on the highways. Through traffic law enforcement, spot checks and increased presence on the highways we make people aware of our presence.'

In Bungay's early days in the Force, people in the rural communities in Saskatchewan were 'super pure and honest – they gave 100% co-operation and would never lie to a cop.' Over the years, as the educational level of the population rose, people became less involved with the police and more aware of their rights. American television provided a great deal of misinformation about police work and citizens' rights. An apathetic public provides a sure shield for criminal activities.

The plight of the victims of criminal activity has become more apparent in recent years. 'The victim suffers so much,' says Bungay. 'With crowded courts, he or she may have to attend five or six sessions before the case is heard, losing time and money each time. The victim is constantly victimized.'

Bungay has increased the Halifax Subdivision's efforts in preventive policing in recent years, although the results of this approach are not easy to measure – as distinct from those from crime detection. A pilot project in police-community relations in Dartmouth and Lower Sackville resulted in the appointment of a full time crime prevention-community relations officer at each post. Each year, Bungay and his staff meet with municipal councils to inform them of what they are doing and to open lines of communication. Under another programme, juveniles are confronted with the consequences of crimes in the presence of their families and the victim, and given another chance rather than being taken to court.

'The deeper people go into the criminal justice system,' notes Bungay, 'the harder it is to get them out.'

The police derive great satisfaction from following a difficult investigation through to its end and seeing justice done. But rewards also come from working with communities to reduce vandalism, juvenile delinquency and drug abuse. At one time, residents of black communities did not dare to be seen even talking to the police. Some Mounties discovered that, in black communities near Dartmouth, there was little for the youth to do. They found the resources to set up a Boy Scout troop, developed a drop-in programme in the schools, and even dug into their own pockets to buy a basketball hoop and ball. The attitudes in the community have changed radically and now members co-operate with the police.

Staff Sergeant Bob Jones, commander of the Halifax detachment, finds detachment work the most enjoyable of all police activities. He joined the Force in 1954 because it appealed to him as a form of public service. He has spent

The RCMP Musical Ride

Women's RCMP uniforms.
Right: Summer dress with long
sleeves and tie.
Far right: Service order of
dress.
Opposite top left: Review
order of dress.
Opposite top center: Review
order of dress with winter pea
jacket.
Opposite top right: Walking
out order of dress.

Men's RCMP uniforms.
Left: Walking out order of dress.
Far left: Review order of dress.
Opposite bottom right: Service order of dress with pea jacket.
Opposite bottom center: Winter dress with parka.
Opposite bottom left: Service order of dress with patrol jacket.

most of his time on detachment work, much of it in Nova Scotia. 'It's a people business. If you are not interested in people, you've chosen the wrong career.'

Detachment work involves the basic police function, he notes: 'You have to be a generalist – it's not specialized, or glorified. You enforce statutes from three levels of government and handle a wide spectrum of duties, from investigating serious crimes to advising citizens. You have to be an amateur psychologist and sociologist – and a sympathetic listener. People often don't know who to turn to when they have a problem.' Citizens will phone up the RCMP to ask about driving conditions and to settle arguments about points of law.

During the 1960s and 1970s, an increasing number of people showed a lack of respect for any rules and regulations, and for anyone who tried to enforce them. 'People have to participate in enforcing law and order,' says Jones. Over the past three years, with the increasing stress on crime prevention by the RCMP, public attitudes have begun to change.

But Jones emphasizes the ambiguous nature of police work:

'You have to retain control of a situation, and stay as calm and collected as you can. Every fatality generates a stressful situation and has an impact on a wide range of people. We have to make sure that we cover every point – the best evidence is the warmest, what you get in the first few hours. It's we and only we who are responsible for reporting the facts. But you must have empathy for people, and try to be a friend.'

One morning a hysterical voice in a small community reported at 6:05 that 'someone drove off the wharf.' The caller was so upset he couldn't remember his own phone number. A member of the Force calmed him down, determined the where and when of the incident, roused the Mountie on call at 6:10, called the local fire department, ambulance and doctor and by 6:50 the victim was out of the water and on the way to hospital.

The Force constantly deals with people who are in need and trouble. 'We have to show a willingness to be helpful outside the limits of our mandate and the law,' stresses Jones.

During 1983, Mounties of 'H' Division brought two operators of a pyramid scheme to court. Constable Morrison told delegates at the annual meeting of the Women's Institute of Nova Scotia how to outsmart rapists. The Dartmouth detachment moved into new offices in Cole Harbour and held an open house. Law students from Dalhousie University served a summer internship with the Force, and five other students made a statistical analysis of the Dartmouth detachment's files and helped to introduce a Neighbourhood Watch Programme. The Force's aerial patrol scanned the highways to identify traffic offenders. Other Mounties investigated a rash of bicycle thefts and a fire that destroyed four fish shacks. The RCMP issued bulletins to newspapers and radio stations to aid in locating tourists sought because of sickness and death in their families. On the South Shore of

the province the Force was called to the scene of an accident where a woman drowned while attempting to rescue two children who had floated away on an inner tube.

Mounties attended university and took part-time courses after duty. Constable Daniel Kelly of Lunenburg and Corporal Joseph Ray of Chester received Medals of Bravery from the Governor-General for rescuing four people from drowning.

And the day-to-day work of the Royal Canadian

Mounted Police went on, just as it has done for 110 years.

Staff Sergeant Bob Jones summarizes the nature of this work that has changed so little since the Force was founded in 1873: 'We work alone. We know and feel that we must act and do our job. We're sustained by a feeling of mutual support, and our history gives us a feeling of total security. The esteem and personal pride that members of the Force feel comes from that – and from the activities of those who have served in the past.'

Above: A RCMP patrol car near Lake Louise, Alberta.
Overleaf: His Excellency Jules Leger, the governor general of Canada, and his wife arriving at Parliament by landau with an escort of members of the Force for the opening of Parliament 12 October 1976.

ACKNOWLEDGEMENTS

In writing this book I received excellent co-operation from the members of the Force whom I contacted. I would like to thank Commissioner Robert Simmonds, Superintendent J R Bentham, Officer in Charge, Public Relations Branch, RCMP Headquarters and Corporal W J (Bill) Kazmel of the same Branch. Chief Superintendent C J Reid, Commanding Officer, 'H' Division, RCMP, Halifax, told me of the work of his division, and arranged for me to meet other officers. I appreciated his help, and that of Superintendent Dave McCormick, Administration and Personnel Officer, Superintendent C A J Bungay, Officer Commanding Halifax Sub-Division, Staff Sergeant Bob Jones, NCO i/c, Halifax Detachment and Staff Sergeant B A Hebb. Joan McNiven helped with the research, and the Halifax City Regional Library again proved its value to writers.

I would also like to express my appreciation to Mr. S. W. Horrall, historian of the RCMP, and author of a standard history of the Force, for his generous co-operation in reading the manuscript and offering comments.

The opinions expressed are entirely mine, and I take full responsibility for them. I'd like to thank the members of the RCMP whom I have met through the years for helping me to understand the real world of their work. Canada is fortunate to have an internationally famous police force whose history, despite recent lapses, should be a source of genuine pride to all Canadians.

Jim Lotz, Halifax.

INDEX

The author and publisher would like to thank the following people who have helped in the preparation of this book: Richard Glassman, who designed it; Thomas G Aylesworth, who edited it; John K Crowley, who did the photo research; Cynthia Klein, who prepared the index.

PICTURE CREDITS
All photographs courtesy of the Royal Canadian Mounted Police, with the following exceptions:
Culver Pictures, 32.
Glenbow-Alberta Institute, 45
McDermid Studios, Edmonton, 107 (top right).
Public Archives of Canada, 118.
Royal Ontario Museum, Toronto, 16-47.
Saskatchewan Archives Board, 106.

SOURCES

The Historical Section of the RCMP issued *A Bibliography of The Royal Canadian Mounted Police* in 1979. It lists almost 1000 references, and can be obtained by contacting the Public Relations Branch, Royal Canadian Mounted Police, 1200 Alta Vista Drive, Ottawa, Ontario K1A OR2. The bibliography contains works critical of the Force, the reports of Royal Commissions, and *The Outlaw Mountie and Red Fang the Wonder Husky*, published in Hampton, Middlesex, in 1937 and surely the ultimate Mountie book. For the early period of the Force's history, R C Macleod's *The NWMP and Law Enforcement 1873-1905* is the best and fairest source, and it is extremely readable. The activities of the Security Service are described in John Sawatsky's two admirable books, *Men in the Shadows* and *For Services Rendered*; they show the human dilemmas of this strange world. The best material on the Force has been produced by those who set down their memoirs in the plain, straightforward manner so typical of the Force's reports. They include *William Parker, Mounted Policeman* (Hugh A Dempsey), *The Horsemen* (C W Harvison), *Without Fear,*

Favour or Affection and *Scarlet and Stetson* (Vernon Kemp) and *Forty Years in Canada* (Sam Steele). In 1973, the Force's historian, S W Horrall, produced an excellent *Pictorial History of the Royal Canadian Mounted Police* and William Kelly, a former deputy commissioner, and his wife Nora wrote *The Royal Canadian Mounted Police*, a factual history that reveals the incredible range of its work. The RCMP issues *The Quarterly* which contains a great deal of fascinating material; it is available to the public by subscription (write The Editor, 'The Quarterly', RCMP Headquarters, Ottawa, Canada, K1A 9Z9). And no understanding of the Force is possible without reference to what Hollywood has done to its image. Pierre Berton deals very effectively with this in *Hollywood's Canada* which contains a chapter on the Mounties and illustrations of how the dream factory has portrayed them. The Archives of the Rockies in Banff contain a photo from *Cameron of the Mounted*, which is not included in Berton's book, but can be bought as a postcard in Banff. On it, Cameron is kissing the heroine, and his three fellow Mounties are kissing their horses! It's hard to determine why so many people chose to distort the truth about the Force when the real work it did is so interesting and vital.